THE COUP

Ken Payne

The Coup

Futura Publications Limited
A Futura Book

A Futura Book

First published in Great Britain by
Futura Publications Limited in 1978

TO SETH AND JOSS
IN MEMORY OF NATHAN

ISBN 0 7088 1359 3
Printed by
William Collins Sons & Co. Ltd
Glasgow

Futura Publications Limited
110 Warner Road, Camberwell,
London SE5

CHAPTER ONE

THERE'S something special about the smells and sounds of a horse yard on a crisp autumn morning, even when it's just a little four-horse yard that's just as much pigpen and chicken run, as mine was on that particular October morning in 1967. The air was cool and wet and pungent, a sweet, heady mixture of damp earth and woodsmoke, of new hay and horses.

In the boxes the lads were chattering away as they bent to their tasks, brushing and polishing, feeding and watering, mucking out the stalls. The chickens clucked about, in and out of the horse boxes, pecking at the ground. Back beyond my New Forest cottttage I could hear the pigs grunting over their morning feed, wallowing in the fresh mud of the autumn rains.

This morning the sun was coming up after the rain, and the overnight hoarfrost glinted on the wet grass as the first bright rays flashed through the stands of beech and elm and oak, ablaze in the red and gold of the season. It was a splendid morning, a morning to erase such burdens of civilization as bank managers and overdrafts and final reminders in windowed brown envelopes. What were bills, what was money, on a beautiful October morning such as this?

Bills were drowning me. Money slipped through my fingers like quicksilver.

But I was hanging on there. I was scheming. I think I

must have been born scheming. A good winner, that's all I needed. One good coup to clout the bookmakers around their earholes. Only how, how to pull off a good 'un and get myself a real stake? I couldn't do it with what I had in the boxes, that was for sure. Not with Harry Flapman, that randy old stallion, not with Portulac, nor with Lark Spring, nor with Skipping, either.

I was standing there in the yard that morning, wondering if maybe I ought to have another go at the window-cleaning business, which I'd just given up. Then Ralph Emery drove up with his pig trailer.

Ralph, one of my good neighbours there at Romsey, was a genius with pigs. He could take a look at a fresh litter, all pink and wet and wriggly like a bunch of fat worms, and point out which would gross up big and flourish, and which would never make the grade. He was always right. Or as near right as made no difference.

Ralph had the same feel for ponies. He could eye a new foal, with its skin still shiny, the little bugger standing there shivering, legs wobbly and splayed, and he could tell you, Ralph could, if it would ever make tuppence at the sales, or ever win a race. If Ralph's wallet had ever been as full as his heart, he might have been a very big man in racing. But Ralph was generous almost to a fault, a real softie. Still, maybe a happier if poorer man for it all.

Anyway, there was Ralph Emery that morning, thin as a fence rail, his normally pallid face flushed with the cold like a rosy apple, deerstalker covering his sandy hair, and his hacking jacket, as always, looking like sixpence worth at the jumble sale. He got out of his old banger that once must have been a lovely Jag, went around back and began to unload the big trailer.

I ambled over. "Got that steeplechaser you were after at Ascot, did you?" I said to him.

"Not exactly." Down the ramp he led a ragged-looking beast, a mean-eyed chestnut as thin as Ralph himself. Seldom had I seen a less handsome specimen.

"What in hell's that?" I said.

"Name's Neronton," Ralph said, looking a bit sheepish. "A gelding."

I shook my head. "Don't tell me you actually paid cash money for this animal, Ralph?"

Ralph slowly rolled himself a Golden Virginia, scraped a Swan Vesta, and lit the fag. He sucked in a deep drag, exhaled the smoke, a blue cloud mixed with his own frosty breath. "I did," he said.

"What the Christ for? What happened to the steeplechaser you had your eye on?"

Ralph sighed. "Well, there was this chappie, you see," he began and then unfolded another Ralph Emery sob story, in which Ralph as usual winds up reaching for his wallet.

This time it was a guy with a hard luck story about a marriage, a divorce and the only thing he had left in the world to sell—his race-horse. It seems this chap had married the boss's daughter, and been made a company director. But it was a door that swung both ways, of course. When she tired of him and kicked him out, the job went out the door with him. He was left with nothing but a batch of solicitors' bills and his beloved gelding, Neronton. Now he had the gelding at the Ascot sales because he just had to raise £350.

All this he had recounted to Ralph Emery, shedding bitter tears all the while.

"Well, I had to help this chappie out, didn't I?" Ralph said to me. "His horse was coming up in the ring before the one I wanted, so I told him I'd help the bidding up to three hundred or so, so's he'd get his price . . ."

"Yeah, yeah." I knew what was coming.

Ralph looked down at the end of his cigarette, squinting at it, as though it held some secret in its glowing ash. "I got stuck with it at three-twenty." He threw the dogend away. "Well, I had to help this chappie out, didn't I?" he repeated.

"I guess you did, Ralph." I shrugged. "What do you want me to do with him?"

"He's supposed to be a hurdler. Give him a few weeks and see if you can make anything of him. If not, I guess he'll have to go to make dog meat."

When Ralph had gone I turned Neronton over to Doug Ward, one of the lads, went back to the cottage and got out the form book. I said to Lynda, who was living with me then, "My God, you ought to see what Ralph Emery's just trundled in. He ain't ever gonna earn his feed, not this one." I thumbed through Timeform and found Neronton.

"I'll be damned," I said aloud. "Listen to this, Lynda. 'Useful high class hurdler.' That scrawny thing out there's won four hurdles, and a selling plate on the flat."

I kept reading, and began to see what had happened to Neronton. His owner, or his trainer, or both, had obviously decided to try to increase his earnings by putting him to steeplechasing. He had been knocked about, fallen a couple of times, and apparently decided that enough was enough—he wasn't having any more of that. Neronton had lost all interest in racing. And much of anything else, to judge by the look of him.

Actually, despite his Timeform history, I didn't have much hope for Neronton. When a horse has hit the ground hard a couple of times and decides he doesn't like it, it's very difficult indeed to get him interested in racing again. But, animals are funny, a lot like humans in many ways. You never know what'll turn one on again to living.

Doug Ward, the stable lad, put Neronton in the one and only vacant box. Only it wasn't quite vacant. The empty box was tenanted by a squatter—a bantam cock we called Fists. Neronton and Fists took up an immediate love-hate relationship that set the whole yard in an uproar. The squawking and whinnying was terrible to hear. When we put feed in the manger the two of them fought like wildcats; feathers and hair and bran flew everywhere. But when we tried to move Neronton out of the box, Fists screeched bloody murder, jumping up and down, flapping his wings, bouncing along scratching at the gelding's heels. If we made a grab for Fists, Neronton would go mad, kick out with his feet, toss his head and snap his teeth viciously.

In calmer moments, Fists perched contentedly on Neronton's back, supervising the scratchings of his harem around the yard, while Neronton munched on his feed. At least he was eating, filling out a bit. At least he seemed to have found some interest in life again, albeit an arrogant little bully cockerel.

But interest in any thing to do with racing, or with anything at all to do with the routine of a racing yard—zero. Neronton just didn't want to know. And as I said, horses are funny, like people, and clever—like some people. Horses know how to malinger if they don't want to race. I remember a mare one time, when I was an apprentice jockey, which went lame every time she went to the race track, but recovered miraculously the moment she got home. Eventually we fooled her by leaving on her work plates when she went to the track, and before she realised where she was and what she was doing she had won by two lengths.

Now Neronton, when I took him out in the morning, wouldn't even canter. No matter what I did to get him going, he ignored me. But as soon as I turned him around and he realised he was heading home to his box and that cockerel, he would set off at a real good gallop.

But a gallop isn't a horse race, and I was getting nowhere with Neronton when Paddy Baldwin paid a visit to the yard. Paddy was stud groom to Lady Bouverie. I'd met Paddy when I was cleaning windows on her ladyship's estate, and we'd become good friends. Paddy was absolutely convinced that most race trainers didn't know a damned thing about the care of horses, especially their feet. He was a complete nut on horses' feet. So when we were walking around the yard and I told him about Neronton, he said to me, "Let me have a look at her feet, Ken."

"Now listen, Paddy," I told him, "I've seen lots of horses' feet in my time, and there ain't nothing wrong with Neronton's. It's his head that wan's looking at, not his feet."

"Just let me look," Paddy insisted.

I let him look. There was no stopping Paddy when he had an idea fixed in his mind. We went into the box, much to the annoyance of Fists, who set up his usual screeching and squawking and fluttering. I shooed him off Neronton's back, and Paddy went around on his inspection tour, humming and sniffing and snorting under his breath. When he'd finished he stood up and faced me. His eyes were wild.

"You need reporting to the R.S.P.C.A.!" he raved. "I don't know how in hell you expect this horse to walk out of his box, much less race. Such feet! The poor thing must be in agony every time he trots!"

I must confess I still didn't see anything wrong with the gelding's feet, but I knew better than to argue with Paddy. If he said he saw something wrong, then something indeed was wrong. Nobody is so smart there isn't somebody just that little bit smarter. Old Atty Persse, greatest trainer of them all, told me that when I was just a two-bob-a-week stable lad for him, and I never forgot it. That's how I picked up a lot of good advice in my lifetime.

I let Paddy go to work on Neronton's feet. I don't know if what he did hurt the gelding, but it certainly pained me to watch him do it. He cut back Neronton's hooves so far they must have been on the point of bleeding. Then he packed each hoof in a kind of poultice made of cow dung, telling me, "Kenny, don't you let this horse out of his box for a week at least. Give those poor feet of his a chance to heal. Don't put shoes on him till then."

When the week had gone by, I had the blacksmith put the shoes back on, and I took Neronton out for a little canter. It was a fine morning, cold and dry, for our familiar amble through the New Forest before the turn for home and a gallop down the side of a field of stubble But this morning Neronton was in no mood for ambling. He took off as though I'd set a blowlamp under his tail. It was all I could do to hold him. By the time I got him back to his box, blowing, lathered, but still full of ginger, I knew I was on to something. A little butterfly of excitement fluttered its wings in the pit of my stomach.

The transformation was unbelievable; from a horse gone sour to a fresh, keen animal, healthy and spirited.

However, the big question remained: would he race? It was time to find out.

We already had a race planned for Neronton, a selling hurdle up north at Catterick. When I'd entered him several weeks earlier, it had been with little hope of actually running him. But the rules require entering a horse some six weeks before a race, so trainers make entries all over the place with lots of horses that will never actually run. You have until eleven a.m. the day before the race to withdraw your horse without penalty. A "late scratch", as a last-minute withdrawal is called, can get a trainer fined.

So I had Neronton scheduled in the kind of race I wanted him to run. And at the track where I wanted him to run. Nobody knew me up north. At Catterick they would treat me as just another trainer who ran his horses for fun and a little prize money, as I did with Harry

Flapman now and again on the southern courses. In any case, nobody knew me anywhere as a "gambling trainer," the kind who made money for himself and his owners by winning bets, rather than prize money, on his horses.

I had never before pulled off a betting coup of any kind. So the situation was perfect for my first one—the one I needed to get myself into the black and set up as a serious trainer. I had the horse. I had the race. But—I knew that Neronton absolutely had to win first time out if I was to score big against the bookies. At Catterick he would be going in at long odds, as befitting his last series of awful races. The moment he began to run, however, everybody would know he was back in his original fine form. If he lost at Catterick, he nevertheless would have run such a strong race that next time out the odds on him would be short; he might even be made favourite.

No, Neronton had to win that seller at Catterick or there'd be no second chance for me. That realisation still left me facing the ultimate question, or, rather, as I thought more about it, two questions. First, would he race. Second, how could I test his reaction to a racecourse after his long layoff, without tipping anybody about his astonishing recovery?

The answer to the first question would have to await the fateful day. However, I could glean an important clue by answering the second question, and I saw the answer to that one coming at Fontwell Park, a week hence.

Fontwell is a neat little track near Bognor, not all that far from my yard at Romsey. Its physical characteristics bear useful similarities to those at Catterick. The bends are tight, the ground uneven and wavy, and there are some tricky inclines. As at Catterick, the boxes are close enough to the grandstands for the horses to hear the roar of the crowds and the Tannoy; these are noises a horse must accept if it's going to be a winning racer.

Another factor that brought Fontwell into my scheme was its reputation as a track for second-class horses. Therefore the more discriminating punters and bookmakers didn't bother to come down for the racing. The last person I wanted to see at Fontwell in a week's time was a sharp-eyed, big-time bookmaker. On that day I had Harry Flapman entered in a selling hurdle. But I intended to bring along Neronton and another hurdler in my string, the filly Skipping.

What I had planned was intrigue. What occurred nearly degenerated into farce.

On the appointed day I packed my three horses into one of Ralph Emery's big trailers, and off I went to Fontwell. Harry Flapman was scheduled for the second race on the card. I put him, Neronton and Skipping in adjoining boxes, and went off to have a flutter on the first race. I dropped a few bob, tore up my ticket and went back to the paddocks to see about saddling up Harry Flapman and checking on the other two. When I got to the paddock area, the security guard ruashed up to me, his face the picture of a man in panic.

"Mr. Payne, sir, thank God you're here! Your horse has got loose and he's in that box over there!" He grabbed my arm and pointed. "Get him out, or we'll all be out of a job!"

I ran over to where a little stable lad was peering over the top of a box door. His mouth was agape, his eyes fairly popping out of their sockets. And small wonder. I looked inside. There was Harry Flapman doing what he was best at—which was not jumping fences. In fact I made more money renting him out for stud than I did running him. Right now, instead of having his mind on racing, Harry Flapman was covering a lovely little mare. Apparently she was in season and Harry must have scented her, jumped right out of his box and into hers.

"What are we gonna do, sir?" stammered the stable lad. "My mare's entered in the next race."

"So's my stallion," I said, grabbing a bucket of water, the tried and true remedy for such situations. I let Harry have a dousing and fortunately it was enough to cool him off. I led him out of the box, slipped the lad a ten-bob note, and said to him, "Forget it ever happened, lad, or we'll both be for the high jump."

Those few stolen moments of love didn't seem to do much good either for Harry or the little mare. She at least finished a respectable fourth. Harry, sulking all the way like a petulant Romeo, trailed the entire field.

When the day's card was finished I asked jockey Ron Atkins if he'd take one of my horses around the course, in what's called "a schooling run." Brian Lawrence would be up on Skipping to keep him company. "Just see how he goes," I said to Ron. "No need to push him if he jumps okay." By now the crowd was well on its way to the car parks. But when Atkins and Lawrence rode out, a few later leavers turned to watch. Most were simply curious; a few, perhaps, were smart enough to recognise a schooling run, and knew that a trainer didn't go to all that trouble just to give his horse the exercise. Still, I wasn't worried about giving the game away. Nobody knew Neronton's identity.

As the horses approach the first hurdle my heart was in my mouth. On his last few times out, before Ralph had brought him, Neronton had either refused or turned around and run the other way. Now he took the first jump without hesitation. I breathed easier. At the second hurdle he went in a length behind Skipping and came out a length in front. By the third hurdle he was flying. "Okay, Ron, okay," I said under my breath. "Bring him back in. He's shown enough!"

But Atkins took him all the way around. When he brought him back to me, Neronton was hardly blowing.

"He's fine, Mr. Payne," the jockey said. "He can really go. What's his name, anyway?"

"Portulac," I said blandly. Butter wouldn't melt in my mouth.

Of course I told Ralph Emery the good news. And I expected that he would confide the glad tidings to a few special cronies. What I didn't expect, but discovered when I arrived at Catterick, was that Ralph apparently had told every pig-farmer and turnip-basher in Hampshire about Neronton. The good folk of Yorkshire must have been amazed at this strange and sudden invasion of New Forest accents.

I knew this meant that the odds would fall on Neronton, but I was hoping that the track bookmakers would take this heavy betting on the gelding as just the misguided loyalty of simple pig-farmers for one of their own, and so would not drop the odds too sharply nor cause the off-track odds to drop too quickly. Since early that morning Lynda had been driving around feverishly, placing small bets in shops everywhere from Southampton to the West End, asking for "board price". That meant we were getting the morning's opening odds "on the board" at the shop, or close enough to it. The "board price" on Neronton was anywhere from 8–1 to 10–1, depending upon the shop. I just hoped Lynda got all our money down before the odds in the shops began reflecting the deluge of New Forest money being bet at the track.

In any case, these "board prices" would have been better than the so-called "starting price" on Neronton. This price is the average of the prices offered and laid on the course at the time the race starts. Since this price is obviously very sensitive to the betting at the track, in Neronton's case his "starting price" was knocked down to 5–1.

Unless a punter in a betting shop specifies "board

price" when he bets, he will be paid off—if he wins—at the "starting price". Since I had something like two thousand pounds bet on Neronton, that difference in odds could mean as much as ten thousand pounds in winnings for me.

Neronton was in the opening race, a £500 selling hurdle. My jockey was Brian Fletcher, who was to ride Red Alligator to victory in the Grand National a couple of months later (and who won it twice more some years later with Red Rum).

In the paddock I gave Brian a few encouraging words, because I didn't think he was overwhelmed with Neronton's latest form—not that he wouldn't give me his best ride just the same. "You'll win it," I said to him. "Just remember there's a fast finish here at Catterick, so hold him for the first few hurdles, then let him out."

Brian nodded. To him, after all, it was simply another race, and a cheap seller at that. To me, it was a beginning—or an end. I had scraped together all I could beg or borrow to pull off this coup. But I couldn't tell my jockey that.

The January afternoon was cold, windy and grey. Yorkshire in winter is never the cheeriest of places. And now, suddenly, I felt depressed. My teeth began to chatter, more from nerves than from cold. I began to doubt the wisdom of my adventure. What the hell was I doing?

As the horses paraded to the post I took hold of myself. At least Neronton looked unperturbed and Fletcher, I knew, had the nerves of a burglar. It could be done. I could pull it off. I took a deep breath, felt better, and rushed to put another fiver on my gelding.

Ralph Emery came over to me then. "Sure hope he wins it, Mush," he said. He always called me Mush, I never knew why.

"Got a few bob on it, eh?" I said, smiling.

Ralph snorted. "Sold every pig I had and bet it all."

My smile vanished. Just what I needed to start my teeth chattering again.

Then they were off. Brian got him out of the stalls sharply, and as the pack reached the first hurdle, Neronton was tucked in neatly behind the favourite and leader, Jungle, ridden by Paddy Broderick. Coming up to the fourth hurdle, down the back stretch, Brian began to move Neronton up smartly.

And then, at the fifth, it happened. Neronton fell.

Clearly, indelibly, as though it was happening in slow motion, we saw him stumble to his knees and Fletcher pitch forward between his ears.

I turned away in shock. I wanted to cry. Ralph put a hand on my shoulder and said to me, "Never mind, Mush. You did a great job. He would have won it. There's always a next time."

Not for me there wouldn't be, I thought. It was back to cleaning windows for a living. "Let's get back to the unsaddling enclosure," I said to him. "Brian'll bring him in."

A couple of seconds later, I was hearing the racing commentator over the Tannoy, only what I was hearing I was not believing.

". . . and it's Neronton coming up fast now as they approach the last, and it's Neronton taking over as they come to the straight!"

Ralph and I stared at each other, incredulous. I was too small to see over the crowd, but Ralph ran up a couple of steps and stood on his toes for a look. "You won't believe it, Mush," he called to me, his arms flapping about in excitement. "He's winning, Mush, he's winning!"

Neronton won, going away.

To this day I have that wonderful photograph of Brian Fletcher, clumps of mud on the front of his cap, leading Neronton into the winner's enclosure. Yes, the gelding had stumbled, but Brian had stayed with him. Neronton had climbed back to his feet, thrown Brian back into the saddle, and taken off after the field. It was a remarkable comeback, and it showed the kind of courage the gelding had.

The aftermath of the race was like one of those Ray Boulting comedy films they used to make at the old Ealing studios back in the 1950's. Ralph Emery and his odd assortment of pig-farmtrs were running around trying to get paid. But the bookies simply didn't have that much cash on hand. They wanted to pay off in cheques, which was normal procedure. Only these lads from the New Forest weren't having any of that. Oh no! Cash on the barrelhead they wanted, and they were getting more than a bit hot under the collar as the bookies tried to stall them off.

Eventually, with the help of the clerk of the course, the bookies got the cash together, much of it in Scottish notes. The New Foresters didn't care for that, either. None of that foreign money for them. They wanted good English pound notes. It took all my powers of persuasion to convince them that the money was good.

They took the cash, although not one hundred per cent convinced. On the way back down the motorway, I had three of them in my car, and they made me stop at every service station along the way to change a few notes and so verify that they were honest paper of the realm.

I was dead tired by the time I got back home, physically and emotionally wrung out. I put Neronton back in his box, where he was greeted raucously by Fists, distributed tips to all the lads, as was customary after a win, and made my way wearily into the house.

There was Lynda, waiting for me. On the table were handbags and carrier bags overflowing with fivers and tenners. Suddenly, I wasn't tired anymore. I felt a tremendous lift of exhilaration. I was ready to take on the whole world of racing. With twenty thousand pounds in my pocket there'd be no holding me. I began to laugh hysterically.

Not bad, I thought, not bad for little Titch from Bassett Green. Pretty damned good, in fact, considering how it all began . . .

CHAPTER TWO

THE VILLAGE of Bassett Green wasn't the safest place to be when the German bombers began to come over in 1940; it was too close to the docks at Southampton. I was born there on a bracing March day in 1937, at No. 2, Poppy Road, the centre house of a cluster of three that stood proudly by themselves with open fields all around. It was a cosy little house, snug and warm, but it seems to me I spent more time sleeping in the Anderson shelter at the bottom of the garden than I did in my bedroom upstairs.

My two sisters slept in the bedroom next to mine. Sonja, eight years older than I, lives today in Salisbury. Sylvia, a year younger, was a beautiful girl. She was crippled, her legs malformed from birth. She was courageous in her suffering and she tried her best, poor little Sylvia. She died when she was thirteen.

When the Battle of Britain intensified and the Luftwaffe hit Southampton day and night, my parents were urged to evacuate us. Sylvia couldn't be moved, however. She needed my mother's constant care. We couldn't all leave; there was no place for us all to go. Besides, my Dad was working on the docks as a stevedore, earning a good wage, and he wasn't going anywhere, bombing or no bombing.

Since under those circumstances it was only fair and sensible that the two girls should stay together, I was the one picked for evacuation. Weepy, but not without a sense of adventure, I was packed up and sent off to Hursley, near Winchester. There my aunt and uncle, Fred and Susan Perrin, had a cottage on the big Chamberlain estate. My aunt worked as housekeeper on the neighbouring estate of Viscount Lifford. Uncle Fred was a chauffeur for Vickers-Armstrong at Hursley Park, where they were making Spitfires.

The memories of my childhood are understandably blurred with time; faded as old photographs. The years, after all, play tricks on the mind, misfile information, make chronology suspect, facts dubious. Memory becomes furtive, hides in dark corners. And yet, there are moments in time etched deeply into the memory; voices, odours, colours, words, entire scenes impressed so vividly that they can be recalled at will as though they had happened the day before.

So I remember a summer's day, when the fields were a sea of green, the sky a sun-bleached blue, and the world an exciting place with American soldiers camped in the woods and a war to stir a child's innocent imagination with heroic fantasy; I remember such a day with crystal clarity. I learned a lesson about myself that day, about who I was and who I wasn't—and indeed who I would never be.

We had an Italian prisoner-of-war on the estate then, a lovely man named Secondo. He lived by himself in a cottage near ours and did odd jobs about the estate. He wasn't under guard. Escape was the last thing in the world Secondo wanted. He hated the war and had come to love England, loved it so much in fact, that after the war he got permission to stay, brought over his wife from Italy, and to this very day runs a farm not all that far from where he was once a prisoner.

He was like a second uncle to me, Secondo. I helped him with his English and he tried to teach me a few words of Italian. I used to follow him around the estate and work with him on his chores when I had no school. One of the things I did for him regularly was water the cows. Troughs were scattered all over the grazing fields, and I had to make sure they were filled with water.

On this summer's day I was filling one of the troughs that stood near an immense wooden gate leading out to an access road. I heard the pounding of horses' hooves, and looked up to see Penelope Chamberlain galloping towards me, her governess at her side. They stopped at the gate. I smiled up at them and bade them good morning. She was a pretty girl, Penelope, a year or two older than I, immaculately turned out in fawn jodhpurs, dark brown riding coat and cap. She was on a beautiful bay, both rider and mount alike reflecting the indefinable yet unmistakable refinement of their aristocratic breeding.

She pointed at the gate with her crop. "Open the gate," she said to me imperiously.

I kept smiling. "Excuse me, Miss," I said to her, "but my Mum taught me always to say please."

"I don't have to say please to you. You're from the cottages."

I turned away from her then and continued filling the trough with water. Behind me I heard the whispering voice of Penelope's governess, and then the voice of Penelope herself, grudging, disdainful, saying to me, "All right then, *please*, if that makes you any happier."

I opened the big wooden gate and let them through, watched them ride off across the field to the road, and I thought, what a rude girl. But somehow I perceived more than that, more than just the rudeness any young lad might expect from any girl about his own age who wanted to cut him, tease him, out of sheer girlish perversity. Of course, since coming to live on the big estate, I had sensed the gap between those who lived in the manor house and we who lived in the cottages. I recognised it, but took little notice. The very young accept the order of things without question, and without resentment. I could romp and play in the fields with the children of Lord Lifford and know, without pique or envy, that I was not one of them.

But now, on this brilliant summer morning, now I did feel the first stirrings of a painful knowledge that there was me, and there was Penelope Chamberlain, and it would always be so. It was almost an unconscious thing, this revelation, a kind of subliminal branding of experience on my young mind.

Looking back, I realise that the first seed of rebellion that was to spur my determination to master thoroughbreds—human and equine alike—was planted there and then. My subsequent skirmishes with the Establishment of the Jockey Club were, I'm sure, manifestations of the resentment Penelope unknowingly instilled in the remote recesses of my mind.

I didn't dwell upon it at the time. Barely understood it, indeed. I simply catalogued Penelope as a stuck-up kid to be avoided in future, and went about finishing my work. I never even told my aunt or uncle about it. I never told anyone about it until now. But years later, many years later, when as a successful trainer I came into contact with grown-up Penelopes and might have, I say *might have*, coaxed one or two into a bedroom, or perhaps into something more, I took that old memory out of my pocket, looked at it and said to myself, "Uh-uh, Ken Payne, that's not your turf." Rejecting them was sweeter vengeance than possession.

They weren't bad years, those pre-teen years of mine. I look back on them fondly; again, perhaps with the nostalgia that comes with the blurring of the images. Certainly they must have been hard times, what with the war, and the bombings, the rationings and the sacrifices. Even after the war I don't suppose we had very much. And the winters, somehow the winters seem to have been so much colder then, with much more snow.

I remember walking two miles through woods ghostly white to the old country school at Otterbourne, and two miles back again, my fingertips and my ears red with cold. But I remember, too, the smell and the warmth of the fire when I'd enter the cottage, and Uncle Fred at the big kitchen table plucking a pheasant he'd poached a few days before. There'd be a hot cup of tea and a buttered scone for me to have by the fire, and I don't suppose there was very much in the world I thought I lacked. I was content.

Sometimes, on an autumn day, the leaves dry and crunchy underfoot, Uncle Fred would take me poaching with him. He never let me shoot, but he'd break open his double-barrelled 12-bore and let me drop the big shells into the breech. Then we'd walk slowly through the silent woods, not a sound but the occasional crow or magpie calling, until suddenly Uncle Fred would stop short, hold up his right hand to halt me, and then whip the shotgun to his shoulder. Sure enough, there'd be a rustling in the undergrowth, then a whir and a flapping of wings and a big beautiful cock pheasant would take wing.

Uncle Fred always let the bird get a flying start before bringing him down. "Fair's fair," he used to say. "If I miss 'em, good luck to 'em." He didn't miss many, but he never shot more than a brace at any one time. The Chamberlains and Lord Lifford were aware of Uncle Fred's poaching. All the men from the cottages poached. As long as it didn't get out of hand it was a tolerated tradition on the big estates. At least, it was in those years.

I didn't know why, but I never cared much for school. I had no serious academic ambitions, although I was better than good in all my subjects. No doubt this was my way of compensating for a complete lack of athletic ability. I was simply too small to be of much use at football or rugby or anything else demanding rugged physical skill. By the time I was sitting for my 11-plus examinations, the nickname Titch was stuck to me like glue.

The war was over now, and there was no reason to stay on in Hursley. I returned home to Bassett Green and entered Bassett Secondary Modern. But I missed country life. Bassett Green, of course, could in no way be imagined a throbbing metropolis; still, it wasn't quite the same as living in a cottage on a big estate.

As often as I could, I went back to Hursley for a weekend. I was there on a Sunday afternoon when my Uncle Arthur and Aunt Ida stopped by for a visit. Their daughter Audrey was with them, a vivacious girl of 19. They'd all come over from Hamptworth, not far down the road, where they'd just bought a pub, called The Cuckoo. Uncle Arthur was tubercular, never in the best of health, and Aunt Ida really ran the place.

"Why don't you come stay a weekend with us, Ken?" she said to me that afternoon.

"Well, I don't really reckon a pub," I said.

Audrey smacked me on the head. "You're not invited to the pub, Titch. But you'd like it around there. My boy friend lives on a big farm and we go riding on weekends. He's got lots of ponies."

"Ponies? Real New Forest ponies?"

"Yes, real New Forest ponies," she mimicked.

That prospect awakened something in me. Riding was a thing I knew I could do well, despite my size, if only I had the chance. And I hadn't watched Penelope and her fellow gentry on the estates galloping about without some of the grandeur of it all rubbing off on me. Learning to to ride would be first rate. New Forest ponies were gorgeous creatures. I was sold on weekends at The Cuckoo.

And so I learned to ride. Every weekend, rain, shine or blizzard, I was up at Hamptworth, riding with Audrey and her boy friend. During school holidays I moved in, lock, stock and old jodhpurs my mother'd bought for me at a jumble sale. It was marvelous sport. Not for a moment did I think of it in any other context, until I had an interview with the Bassett Secondary careers officer in the spring of 1951, when I'd reached the age of fourteen. I don't think I weighed more than five stone at the time.

"Well, what are you gonna do, Ken?" he said to me.

I shrugged. "Hadn't thought much about it, really."

"Planning to work with your Dad, on the docks?"

"Me? I'm too small for any of that."

He smiled. "Yes. Of course. That's why I was thinking, Ken, you've been telling me how good you are at riding ponies and how much you enjoyed it. Why don't you try to become a jockey?"

"A jockey?" For the moment I was bewildered. Such an idea had never occurred to me. I mean, when you're a kid you think about a lot of things you might grow up to be, but a jockey is rarely one of them. At least, it was never on my list, although I was built for it and loved to ride.

"How do you go about becoming a jockey?" I said. Suddenly the idea appealed to me.

"I'm not sure," said the careers officer. "I suppose one writes off to trainers or race-horse owners. Why don't you talk it over with your Mum and Dad?"

I did, that very night. My parents thought it was a great idea. In fact my Dad, who was not exactly a stranger to the bookie at the corner pub (illegal then, of course) was quite taken with the possibility of a jockey for a son. I'm sure his imagination was instantly fired by dreams of inside information and betting coups. Unhappily, by the time I'd reached the Neronton stage of my life as a trainer, Dad had passed on.

He knew a thing or two about horse racing, my Dad, and for his money, the two best trainers in the business were Atty Persse and Tom Yates. That night we sat down and composed letters to both men, at Upper Lambourn and Wantage, respectively, asking if there was a place in their yards for a young, eager lad who loved horses and who could ride.

From Atty Persse came a reply that there was no vacancy at the moment. Tom Yates offered me an interview at once. I went off to Berkshire filled with dreams and expectations. But Tom Yates took one look at me and shook his head. "I'm sorry, lad," he said. "As you may know, I train jumpers. You're too small a lad to handle a big jumper. They take more muscle than I'm afraid you could muster. If you want to be a jockey, best you find a yard where they train the flats."

I was dispirited, but not without hope. Once more I wrote to Atty Persse. I received a reply saying that no vacancy as yet existed, but when one appeared, I would be considered. Came the summer of 1951, and I left school. I didn't want to go on with my education; I now had the single-minded ambition to become a jockey. Weeks went by, however, without a word from Atty Persse. I couldn't remain bone idle, so I took a job with a garage at Thornhill, on the Portsmouth road. I didn't really fancy it, but there wasn't much else to do. My Aunt Ida suggested a job as a farm hand, but farmers needed big strong strapping lads, not the likes of Titch Payne.

The garage job lasted about ten days. There was a girl working there, helping on the pumps, who was very obviously pregnant, and not married. The garage manager kept baiting her, day after day, until I'd had enough of it and told him off. My Sir Galahad stance got me the sack forthwith. The manager took a few shillings out of the till, handed them to me and told me to piss off—only not as delicately as that.

When I got home that night, lower than ever, my mother handed me a letter. "It looks like it's from Atty Persse," she said. I tore open the envelope, unfolded the letter. It was indeed from Atty, telling me that a vacancy had suddenly appeared at his yard, and inviting me to Upper Lambourn as an apprentice.

I jumped up and down like an idiot on a string, waving the letter in the air. "That's it!" I cried. "That's it!"

Two days later I was standing before Atty Persse himself at Kingsdown Stables, my new suit rumpled from the long train journey, my cap twisted in my hands like a corkscrew. I was petrified, and the sight of old Atty did nothing to reassure me. He was an intimidating figure, a very bulldog of a man, about seventy, fierce and glowering. He stood there behind his desk, leaning heavily on two sticks, part of him since taking one too many falls as a steeplechaser many years before. He reminded me a lot of Winston Churchill.

"So you like to ride ponies, do you, lad?" he fairly shouted at me.

"Yes, sir, Mr. Persse."

"Yes, well, you'll have to be showing me a lot of sweat before you'll get a leg up on one of mine. There's hard work to be done around a racing yard, you hear me, lad?"

"Yes, sir."

"Yes, well. Ken, you said your name was?"

"Yes, sir."

"Yes, well, we can't have that. Already have two Kens here. One we call Ken, the other our Ken. We'll have to be calling you something else." He turned then to his blacksmith, Vic Allderton. "What'll we call the lad, Vic?"

"Don't know, guv'nor," Allderton said. "But he sure don't look like no Ken to me. Way he's all togged out he looks more like a duke or somethin'."

"Yes, a duke! That's it then, Vic, we'll call the lad Duke. All right with you, lad?"

"Yes, sir."

So Duke Payne it was. And Duke Payne it still is.

CHAPTER THREE

ATTY PERSSE had the kind of yard that no longer exists in England—more's the pity. He had a string of class horses and class owners. Atty was without question one of the all-time great trainers; he was a trainer of people, as well as horses. His most illustrious discipline was Capt. Sir Cecil Boyd Rochfort, who arrived at Atty's yard in 1906, fresh from Eton, to learn about horses. Eventually Sir Cecil became trainer to King George VI, and continued that royal appointment with Queen Elizabeth II until his retirement in 1968. So being one of Atty's lads was no small thing.

Atty had some thirty horses when I joined him, and seventeen or eighteen lads. We had horses like Durante, Val de Assa, Stephen Paul, Lorelei, Queen of Sheba and Monarch Moore, and Bosky and Casket, two fillies given to me to look after. No lad at Atty's ever got more than two horses. Today some stable lads will get three or four. That's too much horseflesh to handle properly.

The head lad, Archie Hughes, assigned me to a lad named Billy Higgs, and Billy in turn introduced me to the others. Frank Barlow was there then, Tom Townsend, Peter Gomez, Michael Beary and Patrick John Burns, known as "Crow," because he kept a lame one as a pet. Townsend I can safely say was the best lad with a horse I ever met. Today he's travelling head lad for Doug Smith, which means he's in charge of horses in transit and at the track. Why nobody ever set up Townsend as a trainer is a mystery to me; he would be a winner.

Atty ran his yard with an iron hand—and a wooden stick. He'd think nothing of belting you with one of his canes if he felt your morning greeting to him lacked sufficient respect. I've got a scar on my hand where he laid it open one day, and a scar near my left eye where he caught me with his diamond ring after I'd lost my cap in a race. I was none the worse for it—indeed, better for it—and though today I sympathise with many of the grievances of the stable lads, none of them knows what it's like to work for an Atty Persse.

There were no hours. We got up at dawn and worked until Atty was satisfied there was no more to do. Bill Higgs taught me to lay out a horse box in a way you hardly ever see done anymore. Litter was arranged neatly in a corner. New bedding laid down. The horse was groomed immaculately. The tack was rubbed and cleaned and polished till the leather and brass gleamed like new. Then Atty would come around and we'd stand to for an inspection unparalleled this side of the Horse Guards.

For this I got two shillings a week. But working with the horses was just part of being a stable lad for Atty. When your morning's mucking out and inspection was over, you were released for other duties. The more experienced lads would take the first-string horses to the Mandown Gallops for a workout under Atty's appraising eye. These were the horses due to race shortly, and which, therefore, needed Atty on hand to evaluate their fitness.

The Mandown Gallops deserve a few words of explanation. This is a unique stretch of turf on the property of Sir Hugh Nugent, who leases training rights to the stables around Upper Lambourn at so much per year per horse. The ground is given the care of a putting green. It is rich earth that has stood virgin to the plough since time immemorial, and its texture is marvellous. The horses love it.

While the experienced lads who could handle the expensive horseflesh were on the Gallops, the rest of us were put to work around the yard. There was always grass to be cut, a fence to fix or creosote, extra tack to clean, something to repair, an errand to run. Nobody was allowed to idle. I was given the regular task of helping Crow with the boilers under Atty's house, which was centrally heated and had six bathrooms. The boilers took coke, four tons of it every two or three days. There were times down in that dark cellar, shovelling away into the flames, when I felt like a stoker on an old steamship.

For these extra duties I was paid an additional sum of four bob a week.

I'll never forget the time I nearly blew up Atty's house with those boilers.

We were regimented as strictly as any military post at Atty's. Lights out at ten. Two nights out a week—with Atty's prior permission and approval of our social plans. Atty was extremely careful of the reputation of his lads, especially the younger ones. Trouble was a reflection on his yard, and he would have none of that. So I knew that if I asked him for permission to spend an evening watching television with the baker's daughter in town, he would turn thumbs down. This was not Atty's idea of a night off for me.

I decided to sneak out one winter's night. This was not merely a matter of walking off the premises. For one thing, the head lad patrolled at night with a dog. For another, I had those big boilers to look after in the evening. But I made a deal with Crow, whereby he'd cover me on the boilers that night, and I'd do one extra shift for him. At seven on the appointed evening I bellied my way across the fields to avoid being seen, and then took off for Lambourn. Just before I left, I reminded Crow once more about the boilers.

He clapped me on the shoulder: "Not to worry, Duke. Not to worry."

I should have worried.

It was just about ten o'clock when we heard the bells of the Lambourn Volunteer Fire Department clang-clanging their way through town. Everybody went out into the streets. Not much exciting ever happens in Lambourn. I heard somebody shout, "They're headin' for Atty Persse's yard!" I bade a hasty goodbye to the baker's daughter and caught a lift in one of the cars heading out that way.

When we got there I ran to the house. I didn't see any signs of a fire, but steam was shooting out of the windows and from the cellar. The house looked like a kettle gone bersek. Instantly I guessed the story: Crow hadn't seen to the boilers. As I stood there, pondering my next move, a voice said, "Duke must be down there! He ain't in his bed!"

A fireman replied, "If there's somebody down in that cellar he'll likely be cooking like a lobster. Best we get down there and look!"

That's when Archie Hughes spotted me. "Hey, there's Duke!" he shouted. He ran over to me. "Duke, what the bloody hell's happened to the boilers?" he cried.

I looked around desperately for Crow. No Crow. Quickly I explained the situation to Hughes; there was nothing else to do.

He groaned. "Oh my Gawd! Crow's still fast asleep. You know him, a bloody bomb don't wake him up. What're we gonna tell the guv'nor?"

Archie, the fire chief and I rushed into the house then to see where Atty was and what he was doing amid all the uproar. We found him in bed, reading, his bulldog body covered in layers of luxurious fur comforters. He looked to me like something out of *Nicholas Nickleby*. When we rushed in he looked up from his book and stared at us in amazement. The surprise was mutual. The radiators in his room were kicking up a terrific racket, hissing and knocking fit to explode. But old Atty, who was growing deafer by the day, had never noticed a thing, not even the bells still clanging outside his house.

"What the hell do you want?" he thundered at us.

The fire chief explained. Hughes explained.

I never saw Atty so agile before—or since. He came out of that bed like a shot, grabbed one of his sticks and swung it at my head. I think if it had caught me it would have decapitated me. "You stupid little bastard!" he screamed, hopping around after me as I fled for my life. "I'll have your balls for this!" He kept swinging that stick at me like a cutlass as I ducked behind Archie and the fire chief.

"Get him out of here!" he shouted in exasperation, his lethal weapon failing to find its mark. "Get him out of here!" As the three of us fell over each other escaping from the room, I caught Atty's final anguished cry, "You'll pay for this, you little bugger! You'll pay for this!"

I did, too. I was restricted to the yard for a month and had my pay stopped for six weeks.

But I was learning about horses. Atty never let a rap on your knuckles get in the way of your yard work. He was a hard man, a very hard man, yet he saw to it that his lads learned to care for and to ride horses the way those things should be done. Today, with skyrocketing costs, too many trainers are forced to cut too many corners.

I learned what a horse was about, inside out, and I mean that literally. Every evening I washed out the vaginas of my two fillies with warm water; otherwise they'd spend half the night fretting with vaginal itch. When you had the care of a colt you had to wash the penis and lubricate it with oil to prevent irritation and infection.

I learned that the first thing you did when you entered

a horse box, at any time, was to check the legs, especially around the knees, probing gently for swellings. The front legs were doubly important. Problems with back legs were curable, problems with front legs could swiftly end a horse's racing career. The legs had to feel cool to the touch. The slightest sensation of warmth had to be reported at once to Atty.

I learned to examine a horse's droppings for signs of intestinal trouble, to check his teeth, to make sure he was eating all his food. When I began to gallop horses I learned to feel the difference between a horse that was running smoothly and one which was stiff. I got to know when a horse was eager and willing and when it was loafing. I learned that there were horses with "heart", natural winners these, and that there were horses which would never win.

I was working first-string horses on the Gallops three months after I came to Atty. Soon after my fifteenth birthday, he gave me my first apprentice ride, on a three-year-old filly named Mischievous Gillian, in a six-furlong race at Brighton. I finished out of the picture. In fact, I never did win a race as an apprentice jockey, over some fifty rides. I'm not embarrassed by the statistic. There are few around like Lester Piggott, who rode his first winner as a 13-year-old apprentice, riding out of his father's yard just up the road from us. Lester was sixteen when I came to Atty. We'd see each other at the Gallops now and again and got to be reasonably friendly. More about me and Lester later on.

An apprentice normally needs fifty rides or so before he even knows what the hell he's supposed to be doing out there. Figure that out in actual racing time and it comes to maybe an hour's competition, that's all. I mean, Crash! The starting gate clangs open, a pack of horses leaps out in a wild Cossack charge and you're squeezed out, trailing the field and a dead duck, before you've gone two furlongs.

When Atty's wife Emily died in 1953, after a long illness, Atty decided to pack it all in and retire. It came as a terrible blow to all of us, although we should have realised old Atty couldn't go on forever. His departure from racing was a considerable loss; I don't believe the sport will ever see the likes of him again. Atty died seven years later, in 1960.

The yard was gradually broken up. Most of Atty's six horses went to Capt. Peter Hastings-Bass, the rest to Atty's nephew, Jeffrey Brooks. The lads were scattered all over the place. I remained at Kingsdown to the very end. Atty chose me to stay behind with him, Archie Hughes and a couple of others to oversee the last few horses and the stable's final days. This led to a milestone in my life: my first sexual experience.

It was necessary, because of the break-up of the yard, that we few who remained be boarded out. I was taken in by a married woman who lived in a house in Lambourn. She was an attractive woman in her late twenties. She had a daughter of seven, an only child, who immediately took me as an older brother. I enjoyed that role, actually, and we got on just fine.

I soon perceived that the marriage was strained. Often the woman's husband would stay away overnight, or for several days at a time. Why, or where the fault lay, was none of my business. I ate and slept there, rising early to go to work at the yard, returning in the evening.

One afternoon I returned to the house early, I don't remember why, and walked in on a scene that stunned me: there was the lady of the house, naked on the settee, locked in a sexual embrace with a lad from one of the other stables. I mumbled and stumbled and stammered and fled to the kitchen. Moments later she came running in, clad in a kimono, her faced flushed in a mixture of anger and embarrassment. I apologised. She apologised.

"I'm not what you think, Duke," she said, distressed,

her voice pleading. I really didn't know why she cared what I thought, but she went on. "You can't know what it's like, Duke. You're just a boy. But my husband and I, we . . . " She burst into tears. I didn't know what to do.

"You want a cup of tea?" I said.

She nodded, smiling through the tears.

I brewed a pot of tea, and we sat there in the kitchen, in silence, drinking tea and munching biscuits. After a time I got up and said to her, "I have to be getting back to the yard."

"Yes," she said. She put her hand on my arm. "Duke? You won't say anything . . . ?"

"Course not." I felt somehow older, wiser, being in the possession of this older woman's secret, becoming, in effect, her confidant, her co-conspirator. I confess I was also not a little aroused. The imprint of her naked body, those naked bodies entangled on the settee stirred me disturbingly.

Several nights later, as I lay in my bed listening to the radio, I heard voices downstairs, voices raised in anger. I turned down the radio and tiptoed to the door of my room, opened it a crack, listened. I recognised the voice of the woman's father. He was shouting terrible abuse at her, calling her a whore, threatening to tell her husband of her shameful indiscretions with this stable lad, to have her daughter taken away from her if there was a divorce.

She pleaded and cried, to no avail. He told her he would expose her to the whole town, to all her friends, have the lad sacked. He threatened her with just about everything but burning at the stake and eternal damnation.

I heard the front door slam, and then only the sound of her weeping. I put on a robe, checked down the hallway to make sure the little girl was still asleep, and went downstairs. She was sitting on the settee, that cushioned altar of lust, crying her heart out.

"Cup of tea?" I said. It was all I could think of, sixteen-year-old jackass that I was.

"Oh?" Obviously she hadn't heard me enter. "Oh, it's you, Duke. Yes, please."

I padded to the kitchen, returned a few minutes later with tea and biscuits. She was still sobbing desperately. "I'm going to kill myself, Duke!" she cried suddenly. "What else can I do now? I'm going to kill myself!"

This was making me very nervous. I didn't know how to handle something like this. She wouldn't stop crying. I had to hold the teacup for her to sip from. I tried to quiet her, afraid she would wake the little girl. She just sat there, moaning, holding herself, rocking back and forth. "You won't leave me, will you, Duke?" she said abruptly.

"Me? Well, I ain't going nowhere, not for a few more weeks, anyway."

"No! You mustn't go away!" She began wailing again. Finally I persuaded her to go to bed. I went back to my room, my mind in turmoil. I slept fitfully.

In the morning she wouldn't let me go to work. She looked a frightful wreck, her face drained of colour, eyes bloodshot as though she hadn't slept a wink, hair in disarray. I was concerned for the little girl. I promised her I'd help get the girl off to school, and then we'd see. But I couldn't escape. She said she's kill herself if she was left alone. She said she'd pay me to stay, give me anything, but I mustn't leave her alone.

I telephoned the yard, spoke to Archie Hughes and told him I was feeling out of sorts, needed the day off. And so began an insane week, a week that began in a nightmare and ended in a delicious dream.

I was a prisoner in the house. She wouldn't, or couldn't, do a thing. I took complete charge of the little girl. I cooked and cleaned. Archie kept calling me and I kept telling him I was sick.

She never got dressed, the woman. She spent half the

day and night crying. I didn't know where her husband was. She wouldn't let me call her father. She was in such a state that toward the latter part of the week I even had to bathe her. It was a natural thing, the way it came about. She walked about as though in a trance, and I cared for her as I would a baby. I washed her, dried her, put her to bed and brought the usual cup of tea.

She drank it and said to me, "Stay with me, Duke."

I wasn't quite sure what she meant. "I've been here, all week."

"I mean now," she said. "I'm afraid to be alone. Stay with me tonight."

I can say with complete honesty that, considering the state she was in, I never thought she wanted anything but a body in bed with her, a human to give her comfort and company. Naive? Perhaps.

I slid into the bed, careful not to make contact. I reached over to switch off the bedside lamp, but she said, "Leave the light on, Duke. I don't like the dark."

I settled myself comfortably, closed my eyes, and tried to forget where I was. Being in bed with a woman was a strange and unnerving experience. After a time, no more than a few minutes, I felt her moving against me, felt a hand on me, fingers, searching. Her warm breath was on my face, her voice, in my ear, was saying softly, "Have you ever been with a woman, Duke?"

Panic seized me. Christ! I thought. This was it!

"No," I said. "Never."

Her fingers found my erection, her lips found mine, her tongue filled my mouth . . . and she led me, led me all the way. I was too quick; I became flustered, shamed by my quickness, but she waited, patiently, and then she led me once again, more slowly this time, and yet again, in the small hours of the morning, until we fell asleep in each other's arms, exhausted, satisfied, fulfilled.

When I woke up the next morning I thought, wryly,

well, Ken, you've broken your maiden at last, though not on top of a race horse.

For two days and two nights we drifted in erotic euphoria, hardly bothering to get out of bed except to make sure the little girl was dressed and fed and properly cared for. We were discreet when she was about; we didn't want her to know, although she realised, obviously, that something in the house had gone wrong.

I felt then, and I feel to this very day that there was nothing sordid about our affair. It was beautiful, as only a relationship between a young man and an older woman can be. I loved that woman for what she taught me, did for me in those few days. And I know that I filled a need for her, at a most desperate time in her life.

Still, it couldn't continue. I had to return to the yard. She let me go, when a week had passed; after all, I'd be returning every evening. At least until Atty disposed of the rest of the horses. After that—we didn't talk about after that.

When I arrived at the yard that morning Archie Hughes said to me, "Guv'nor wants to see you, Duke."

"What about?"

He leered at me. "You know what about."

I was for it now. Nothing less than the wrath of God would descend upon me. Gingerly, I entered Atty's office, stood before him, bracing myself for the blows. He was sitting in a big leather chair, his eyes baleful.

"Is it true, Duke, what I hear? About you and that woman?"

My mind raced about, searching for wild lies. Couldn't find any. I nodded. "It's true, guv'nor."

To my utter consternation, he began to chuckle. "Yes, you're one of my lads all right, Duke. One of my lads."

However, he told me, rightly, that it shouldn't continue. She was still a married woman. There was a child in the house. Tongues were wagging. If it got back to him, then half of Lambourn must know about it. This was no good for me, no good for the woman, no good for the reputation of Atty Persse. So, forthwith, he was sending me to Bob Read, who had a yard nearby. But at Read's there would be living quarters for me, and I would be restricted to the yard for a time, to let the affair cool off.

And that's the way it was. To this day, although a lot of water has flowed under a lot of bridges, that woman and I stay in touch, and remain good friends. Just friends.

Going from Atty Persse's yard to Bob Read's was like leaving Harrod's to work in Woolworth's. This is not to deprecate Bob Read, a brilliant trainer. It's just that while Atty had some of the best horses in Britain, Bob had some of the worst. This had a most salutary effect on my education. By now I was beginning to have doubts about a career as a jockey. I sensed that I was an efficient, though not inspired, rider. But more worrying was my weight. I was a growing boy, in all directions. To stay at seven stone ten meant for me a starvation diet: breakfast was dry toast and black unsweetened coffee; lunch a bit of lean meat, a few sprouts or a bit of cabbage; dinner boiled fish and a small salad.

The thought had occurred to me, therefore, that I might aspire to become a trainer. I was good with horses, I liked the atmosphere of a yard. I knew it would take many years before I could hope that someone would trust me with a horse, and that I might never make it, might never get to be more than a head lad. Still, at sixteen, one can dream, and if nothing else I had confidence in myself.

If training, rather than riding, was to become my career, then there wasn't a better school for the likes of me than Bob Read's yard. It seemed to me then, and nothing I experienced later changed my thinking, that unless a trainer had first-class connections with wealthy owners he didn't get Derby-class or Grand National-class horses. This meant that for the most part he was training horses that raced for peanuts in prize money. For every Noel Murless or Fred Rimell there were ten Bob Reads trying to sneak across a winner so they could cash a bet and pay the wages bill.

Bob introduced me to the world of the "gambling" trainer. He was surrounded at Lambourn by such big-time trainers as Keith Piggott, John Bisgood and Fulke Walwyn. He survived by renting out some of us as jockeys to these trainers, for a fee, by keeping one barn filled with battery hens as a sideline—and by pulling off the rare betting coup with one of his cheap platers.

His horses were bad enough; Bob had a way of making them look even worse at the track. He'd throw a big old blanket over the animal and dress it up in some awful gear till it looked like a circus donkey—all within Jockey Club rules, of course. He would run the animal in races hopelessly out of its class or distance. And then, sometime during the year, he'd spot the right race for it, get his best rider on it, spread his money around with the off-track bookies to keep the price long, and win himself a grand or two.

If being apprenticed to Atty was like being sold into slavery to Hitler (I joke; I loved the old guy) then working for Bob Read was like waltzing with Mary Poppins. It was a lark. He was a grand chap, Bob, tall, slim, red-faced and white-haired. He was about sixty then, I guess. But we lads gave him more headaches than his horses. When he was off somewhere at the races, we made ourselves at home in his house. We smoke his cigars, listened to his records, drank his beer and used the old Ford he'd leave behind. Once, one of our escapades with the Ford got a little out of hand. When Bob returned home from the races that night, he found it upside down on a dungheap.

"Damn those gypsies!" he said. He never suspected

that we took advantage of his good nature, poor Bob.

The *Daily Sketch* ended all of this for me. I daresay Fate interferes with all our lives, some more, some less; some for better, some for worse. External forces beyond our control constantly push us around, often altering the course of our lives dramatically.

The *Daily Sketch* decided, early in 1955, that too many professional sportsmen were being deferred from National Service. They ran a campaign against this practice, singling out Mike Hawthorn as a prime culprit. Mike was abroad racing for Ferrari at the time. The *Sketch* campaign had its effect. Deferments for professional athletes were cancelled. Shortly afterward I got a letter from the War Office saying I was subject to a call up, and would I report to Bugle Street, Reading, for a physical examination.

I was not amused. I am as patriotic as the next man and would have gone off to fight Hitler and the Japanese waving the flag and willing to give my all. Really. But I didn't see what a Communist insurgency in Malaya had to do with me. No doubt I was ignorant and short-sighted; I never claimed to be an expert in geo-politics. I was just a five-foot, seven stone ten, stable lad and sometime jockey who knew damn all about the world outside racing. But the day I got that awful letter from the War Office, I stripped off, looked at myself in the mirror and said out loud, hoping somebody up there would hear me, "What the hell can they use this for?"

The doctors at Bugle Street reacted similarly. The first one to greet me said, "But you're so bloody small!" The next one laughed and said, "A pack and rifle weigh more than you do!" I was much encouraged by all this medical raillery about my physical proportions, or rather lack thereof. Which shows how little I knew about the Army. A week later I got another letter telling me I was graded A1—accepted. I was ordered to report to Winchester Barracks within twenty-one days. Included was a travel voucher and a meal ticket.

It served me right for being healthier than Bob Read's horses.

Just before I left for Winchester I went around for a farewell drink with old Atty Persse. "You'll do all right, Duke," he said to me. "You survived Atty Persse's yard, you got nothing to fear from the Army."

CHAPTER FOUR

THE OFFICERS and men of the Royal Hampshire Regiment were as amazed to see me as I was to finding myself at Winchester Barracks. I heard mutterings about "... sending us midgets," and ". . . scraping the bottom of the barrel." My predicament was made even more ludicrous when I reported to Quartermaster's. They had no uniform to fit me. Not a stitch. I was assigned a place in the barracks, told to report to a Sergeant Kincogan, and assured that I'd be notified when gear was found for me.

Sgt Kincogan didn't believe I was real. He was quite sure somebody was having him on. "What the bleedin' hell am I supposed to do with you?" he roared, when finally convinced I belonged to him. "This here's an infantry regiment, not Billy Smart's bleeding' circus!" He absolutely refused to let me start training without a uniform.

"What can I do, then?" I said to him.

"You can get up every morning at half past bleedin' five like the rest of us!" he said, choking on his wrath. "And then you can get your arse over to bleedin' sick parade, that's what you can do!"

That's exactly what I did. Each morning when the bugle sounded Reveille I'd curse and moan and stagger out of bed with the rest of the men in the barracks. I'd dress in my civilian clothes, stand parade, announce myself present and accounted for, and then, while the rest went off for training, I reported to the medics. It was all a huge joke in the regiment. I couldn't have cared less and, at the back of my mind, harboured a secret hope that the Army would get fed up and give me my walking papers.

No such luck. After three weeks of sick parade, my uniform arrived, and I was thrust into infantry training with the rest of my company. Everybody thought I'd collapse under the sheer weight of my kit and rifle, and I suppose under my helmet and full pack I must have looked somewhat like a deformed turtle. But old Atty called the turn, as usual. There was nothing the corporals, the sergeant or the Regimental Sergeant Major could throw at me that I couldn't take—bless them all.

Mind you, I was not a model soldier. I admit it. Somewhere within me lurked a maverick spirit, constantly alert, waiting to break out. As I said, I must have been born scheming. I dodged heavy duty when I could. Twice I went over the wall to Salisbury to bet on the races. The RSM, a beefy, red-faced Irishman named Watten, did his nut trying to keep me in line. There was one particular oak tree on the parade grounds he considered his "punishment tree". For minor infractions he'd have a man double around it with full pack and rifle for five minutes or so. That big old tree and I were soon fast friends.

I don't know how many times Watten shouted at me, "Payne, I'll have you on the double around that tree till you'll think you're runnin' through bloody Sherwood Forest!"

There was some ten weeks of this. Despite my distaste for the military, pride made me good with the tools they gave me. I could handle my .303 Enfield, a Sten gun and a grenade as well as any, and help hump a heavy weapons vehicle across rough terrain better than any lorry driver with ten years up the M1.

When our training period was over, we were moved to Southampton and loaded on a troopship called the *Empire Orwell*, bound for Malaya. What a tedious, boring trip it was, packed like sardines into stifling holds. We whiled away the long hours playing cards, cleaning our equipment over and over again, and listening to lectures about CT (Communist Terrorist) tactics in Malaya. Few of us actually understood what this so-called Malayan Emergency was all about, but apparently it had been going on since 1948 (and didn't end until 1960).

The way I got it was something like this: apparently a small group of Malay Communists, probably Chinese, who had fought with us as guerillas against Japan during World War II were now under orders from Moscow to stir up trouble. There weren't very many of them, it wasn't a full-scale revolt as in Vietnam, but in the Malayan jungle just a few men could make an awful lot of trouble.

The CT's used hit-and-run tactics, ambushes, assassination. They sabotaged tin mines, burned rubber plantations, terrorized native villages, destroyed convoys. There were already substantial British forces in Malaya, including six Gurkha battalions, but still more were needed. As armies and governments have discovered since the beginning of warfare, when you fight guerillas on their home ground, you seem to be needing a sledgehammer just to crack a walnut.

We docked eventually at Singapore, and it was there, at debarkation, that a medical orderly noted I was not fit for duty. Because I missed my first three weeks of training, I also missed a sequence of inoculations necessary for any man posted to the Far East. There were a few moments' discussion about sending me on to Korea with the ship, a thought that horrified me, or sending me back to England, a thought that delighted me. But nobody appeared willing to make a decision. Finally a compromise was worked out, to wit: I would be unloaded at

Singapore but put directly into the Base Military Hospital until I'd had all my shots. Back on sick parade I went, indefinitely.

In the slang of the American soldier, I never had it so good. I found a home at the B.M.H., with little to do, good food, pretty nurses and a couple of race tracks nearby to fatten my meagre Army pay packet. I even found a way to make extra money running errands and doing odd jobs, sometimes for the nurses, sometimes for the American G.I.'s, most of them recuperating from wounds suffered in Korea.

It was lovely. I was like the mascot of the hospital. Little "Dukey" Payne was so useful to have around. I was getting my shots all this time, but there was no word about sending me on to active duty. I certainly didn't make any enquiries on my own. I was perfectly content to spend the rest of my National Service right there in Singapore and leave the CT-chasing to my old buddies of the Royal Hampshires. I didn't want to kill anybody.

Being me, however, I inevitably got into trouble at that hospital, sooner rather than later. And over a girl; a nurse, an officer in the Queen Alexandra's Royal Nursing Corps. Her name was Kate, and she was from Jersey. I had run errands for her before, many times. This particular morning she asked me to take her skirt into town to the dry cleaner's; it was her best dress skirt, grey-green with full pleats. It was vital that the skirt be returned that afternoon because she had some sort of formal do on that evening, an officer's dance I think it was.

As I was leaving for town, some American G.I.'s I knew waylaid me. "Hey, Dukey boy, how about a game of cards?"

"Can't," I said. "Got to get this to town to be dry-cleaned right away."

"Hey, forget it," one of them said. "We got our own laundry. Beats anything they got in town. We'll have it cleaned, wrapped and ready for you in plenty of time."

Why not? I handed over the skirt and went off with them for a friendly poker game. They played devilish varieties of poker, these American soldiers, with all sorts of wild cards. And they earned so much more money than we did, that their "friendly" game was to me a very high stake one. I didn't mind, because I usually won.

After the mid-day meal, I returned to my quarters for a bit of kip. I was awakened by a Chinese. He shoved a package at me, neatly wrapped in brown paper. "Lady's skirt," he said, bowing. "G.I.'s say all done."

I gave him a couple of coins and sent him on his way. Damned efficient, these G.I. laundries, I thought. I got up, dressed and went straight to the nurses' quarters. By now I was so well known around the hospital that I came and went more or less as I pleased. I didn't even bother to knock at the door to the nurses's quarters, but went straight in and to the room shared by Kate and another nurse. I knocked there, of course. Kate answered. Proudly I handed her the package. "Back in record time," I said airily.

"How much was it?" she said.

I waved my hand. "On me. I had a good day fleecing the Yanks at poker." What the hell, I could afford to be generous. The Yanks had done it for free.

I strolled back to my quarters, stopping off for a cup of tea in the kitchen. By the time I got back I found two warrant officers waiting for me—male. One was a pink-cheeked lad about my tender age, the other sported a Guards moustache and looked as though he'd been born in a uniform, would die in a uniform, and would refuse to take it off even for St. Peter—or the devil, for that matter. He turned out to be the spokesman for the two.

"Payne?"

"That's me."

"Payne," he said, "I suppose you think you're pretty funny."

I hadn't a clue what he was on about, and told him so. Only then did I notice that Pink Cheeks was carrying what appeared to be Kate's laundry package. I pointed to it. "Anything to do with that?"

Sneers from the pair of them. "As if you didn't know," said Pink Cheeks. He opened the package, removed the contents, held it up for me to see.

I gasped "Holy Christ!" I breathed. It was Kate's skirt all right, cleaned and perfectly ironed. Too perfectly ironed. Every single pleat had been pressed out. The skirt was as flat as a pancake. And starched!

"It's a mistake!" I said.

"You bet it is," said Moustache. "Yours, me lad. Let's go." He grabbed me by the bicep and squeezed. I winced; it was like being clamped in a vice.

"Where we going?" I stammered.

"To see the major."

Major Who I didn't bother to ask; I was in it now for sure.

They hustled me between them out of the ward, back to the nurses' quarters and into the office of a major in the Nursing Corps. I stood to attention, hoped for the best, looked at the major, and expected the worst. If there existed an ounce of the milk of human kindness in her, it was not evident on her face.

"Private Payne," she opened without preamble, "you are here on serious charges."

"What's so serious?" I began. "I mean it's only—"

The major banged a baton on the desk. "Quiet! You'll speak when asked to, Private Payne!"

She motioned with her head to the Escorts. Pink Cheeks went to the door, opened it, and ushered in Kate. She was dabbing at her eyes with a handkerchief.

The major jabbed her baton at me. "This the man?"

she said to Kate, who nodded, sniffing.

The major then began to read me the riot act: wilful destruction of Government property, insulting an officer, disregard of military regulation numbers so-and-so and etcetera. I stood there in disbelief. What a load of old cobblers, I thought to myself. All this over a skirt?

When the major had finished her recital of the dastardly crimes of which I was accused, I figured I was good for six months at least in the "glass house". But Kate came to my rescue. She really didn't want to press charges. She accepted that the laundry had been in error, and that I'd intended no offence. She had made the fuss in the first placc, she explained, only out of shock and surprise at opening the package. She went on to praise my character and aver that until that incident I'd always been of the most scupulous behaviour and of great value to many of the nurses.

With apparent reluctance, the major agreed to heed Kate's pleadings. There would be no court-martial. But I would be taught a lesson, nevertheless.

"Since the laundry business seems to be a regular sideline of yours, Private Payne," said the major, "very well, you can do laundry. For two hours, every day, for the next two weeks, you will report to the nurses' quarters and be given ironing to do!"

What a storm in a teacup. No wonder we lost the Empire.

But that wasn't the end of it. Apparently the whole business was good for laughs around the officers mess and perhaps it was inevitable then that some eager paper-pusher should take a squint at my file to find out who I was and what I was doing ironing nurses' uniforms at the hospital.

In quick time, my sinecure evaporated. My inoculations now being in order, I was forthwith posted to my unit, which was up north in Kuala Kubu Bahru. Bandit country. I wasn't pleased about that. I wasn't pleased about that at all.

On my way up to join the Royal Hampshires I had to stop at a village called Nesoon. This was a transit camp for everybody going north. Once you got out of Nesoon you were likely to be hit by a CT ambush at any time, so all travellers stopped there to pick up an armed convoy. Sometimes you waited a day, sometimes a week or more, depending upon how active the CT were at any given moment.

I fell into a bit of good luck for a change at Nesoon. While officers, as was their privilege, were given reasonable accommodation, all other ranks camped out in the "bashers"—tents. As it happened, I came up to Nesoon on the train in the company of a nurse from the hospital. Since we arrived together, the corporal who was assigning quarters assumed I was a medical orderly travelling with her, and put me in Nesoon's only hotel, with other medical personnel. Of course I did nothing to disabuse him.

It was just as well. On my second day at Nesoon I came down with something. Exactly what, I don't know, but I suspect that I had already contracted malaria. I had the shakes, I was feverish, I was nauseous. Yet I didn't dare go on sick parade. Not again. They wouldn't believe me. Not only that, I was on the edge of the combat zone where contracting malaria was a court-martial offence, catalogued as "self-inflicted wounds," like bad sunburn or V.D. True enough, there were chaps who didn't take their anti-malaria Palladrin tablets, either out of neglect or, in rare cases, in an attempt to get themselves out of the danger zone. Still, I never actually heard of a malaria case standing trial.

I figured that whatever I had, I would sweat it out in the hotel. Maybe it was just a passing thing. The heat, the humidity, the food—any of these or a combination of them could be causing what I had. Or so I rationalised. After all, I'd been fully inoculated, albeit belatedly, and took all my pills every day—well, *almost* every day.

The shakes came and went like the tide. When they washed over me I could do nothing but lie in bed and suffer. When they receded I felt fine, with no after-effects. I told my friendly little nurse about them, hoping she could help unofficially. And, I suppose, I was fishing for a little loving sympathy. Of course, she was an officer, but she was a cute little thing and I never did worry too much about the military code of conduct.

She understood my insistence on staying off sick parade. Or maybe she misunderstood. She knew my history at the hospital, and so I assumed she realised that further appearances by me would be viewed with suspicion. But she may have wrongly translated my ducking trouble for seeking action. She may very well have thought I wanted my crack at the CT, silly girl that she was.

She was silly, too. Had we been caught together, it would have meant maybe thirty days in the glass-house for me. For her, it would have been dismissal from the Service. Just the same, we both threw caution to the winds. Maybe it was the spell of the soft tropical night and the hot yellow moon and the jungle fragrances that did it; languid, lusty sex out of a Somerset Maugham story. Certainly, there was no boozing involved. The only alcohol we had was the rubbing fluid she massaged into my feverish flesh. The effect this had on me was soon apparent. I did nothing to hide it. Her hand was drawn to me like an iron bar to a magnet; or, in this case, like a magnet to an iron bar . . .

"I thought you were feeling poorly," she said, smiling.

"I'm ill," I said. "I'm not dead."

She stood up and began removing her clothing. I was not the shy young virgin this time. I watched her openly, enjoying the casual strip. She had a lovely body, petite and shapely, with breasts like two small creamy pears.

When she was naked she slid her body on top of mine, wriggling like a snake, her skin cool against me. Her tongue slithered into my ear and then she said, laughing deep in her throat, "Better go easy, Dukey. Remember, you're weak as a lamb."

"Right now," I said, "I feel like a bull."

I performed like one, too.

We were fortunate, she and I. Fortunate that we were never caught, and fortunate that we got stuck in Nesoon for ten days while we waited for an "armoured bastard" This was the name given to a heavily armed and armoured steam engine that preceded all trains north out of Nesoon by some one hundred yards. Its purpose was to clear the rails of mines and obstructions and take the brunt of any ambushes set by the CT. At the time I was in Nesoon an attack had put one of these "armoured bastards" out of action, and so we awaited the arrival of another.

It arrived; our idyll ended. I was feeling better. I hadn't had an attack for several days. Maybe sex was the cure for whatever it was that ailed me. In any case, my nurse was going up the coast to Ipoh, while I was due to get off earlier, at Kuala Kubu Bahru. I think, in the end, we were glad our paths took separate directions. The party was over.

Up at Bahru, as we called it, the party was over indeed. Life was taken very seriously, because if you didn't you were quite likely to lose it. I joined a company of Royal Hampshires attached to the Royal Engineers. Together we took Advanced Jungle Warfare Training, and then we were subject to call for regular patrol and ambushes. We were turning the tables on the CT, trying to beat them at their own game.

It was no fun. You spent days marching out into the jungle and days marching back again, often without ever seeing an enemy. You spent more time fighting leeches, mosquitoes, dysentery and tenea than you did fighting the CT. Tenea is diabolical. It's a kind of ringworm, or jungle rot, that gets into your skin and makes it itch so madly you just want to grab a razor and scratch, scratch, scratch your skin away. On your feet it was bad enough; if you got it in the armpit or in your crotch you went stark raving bonkers. You couldn't wear clothes. Modesty in any case goes out the window in the Army, but at Bahru if you got tenea in the crotch you walked around "with your dick in a sling" and you didn't care who saw you.

Then there was the rain. England's like the Sahara compared with Malaya. Up at Bahru if it wasn't raining then it had just rained, or it was just about to rain. Everything was mildewed and mouldy. Including the food, which, of course, was as bad as could be expected under the circumstances. I ate so many tinned peaches that to this day I can't stand the sight of one. We used to say, up at Bahru, with just a bit of soldierly exaggeration: When you first arrive and find maggots in your bread, you throw it away. A few weeks later you're picking out the maggots and eating the bread. In six months' time you're eating it all and saying, "Mmm, fresh meat!"

After a time I was sent back to Kuala Lumpur for a radio course. Five wonderful weeks of clean beds, dry clothes and edible food. I was taught Morse code and the use of a new, lightweight shortwave radio, about the size and weight of a small TV set. It was, nevertheless, no fun lugging that thing around in a steaming jungle, and why they picked the smallest and scrawniest man in the company to hump it I'll never know. Because of the radio on my back I couldn't carry a rifle, so I was given a .38 pistol and a giant of a man named John Ovigni to ride shotgun on me. Patrol in the jungle was single file: I was always last but one in the file, with John behind me, guarding me and the radio. He did actually carry a shotgun, which is a very handy weapon at close quarters in jungle fighting.

One day the word came down to get ready for a full-scale patrol and ambush. When that happened, as it did now and again, half the company would arst go into the bush with the local girls, just in case it was for the last time. (Actually, I don't recall even one of my company getting killed.) Many of the local Malays were quite pretty, and the cost of a quick one in the bush was two Woodbines.

Our ambush point on this occasion was a tin mine, a day's march away. We'd been tipped off that some CT's planned to sabotage the mine and kill a few Chinese labourers, hoping to scare the rest of them into leaving the mines en masse. We got to the rendezvous point and into position. There was a full company of us, plus a platoon of Gurkhas and some Dyak trackers. The tin mine was on an island in the middle of a big lake. On our side of the lake, where we deployed, a narrow-gauge railroad line led down to a quay where barges would bring the ore from the island for loading into ore trains from the smelter.

We formed an arc around the lake, leaving the area around the railroad track open. We had been told that the CT's would be coming down the track and crossing the lake to the island in small boats.

For a day and a half we waited, hidden in the jungle, hardly daring to move. Those CT's had noses like bloodhounds and could smell out an ambush a mile away. We were never allowed to use hair tonic, scented soap or even civilian toothpaste up there, because it would give us away. The more we smelled like rotting vegetation the safer we were, and believe me, that's just about how we all smelled up at Bahru.

As usual, our information was wrong. After thirty-six

hours' lying in wait for the CT's to arrive, we discovered that they were already there. One of the Dyaks had swum across to the island and found out that the CT's had arrived there hours ahead of us and were merrily destroying equipment, stealing food and terrorizing the Chinese miners. There were, he thought, about six of them. Once again it was the old sledgehammer to crack a walnut.

That night the CT's decided to leave. They probably knew we were awaiting them because they shot out all the big night shift floodlights on the island and began to make a hell of a racket. There was a moon, and at night in the jungle everything is bathed in a strange glow due, I think, to phosphorescent plants and insects. Anyway, around midnight it fell suddenly quiet. We waited, eyes straining in the darkness. I was lying in some deep grass with Ovigni, hoping that whatever happened, it would be on the other side of the lake. The trouble was, I was too close to those damned railroad tracks.

Suddenly, hell broke loose. I heard running feet, a shout, and then firing began all around me—rifles, then a Sten opened up somewhere to my right. I hugged the ground, whispered to Ovigni, "Keep that bloody shotgun handy!"

Running feet came closer, and then almost stepped on me. I felt a foot hit the ground at my side and sensed a body leaping over me. Whoever it was stumbled over Ovigni and kept right on going. Ovigni cursed, rolled over and leg go a blast with his shotgun, murdering a bunch of leaves and starting a terrible ringing in my ears.

Another rattle of small arms fire, more shouts, curses, a scream, and then silence again. The whole thing lasted maybe five minutes. I could hear men moving around, rising from the ground. I stood up and walked toward the railroad tracks, where a small knot of men was gathering. I joined them and saw, at their feet, the body of a CT, perhaps the very one who had almost stepped on me a few moments before. His body was absolutely riddled with bullets, his green jungle fatigues ripped to shreds, his green cap with the red star in front stained with blood. Incredibly, he was still alive, though the blood leaked from him like water from a colander.

We recovered three CT bodies and found a trail of blood leading into the jungle, indicating at least one more wounded. None of us suffered a scratch.

Several weeks later we were given the word that a big push was coming up. We were going to mount a giant sweeping operation in regimental strength from the central highlands to the western beaches. As we advanced, the Navy was to move in off the coast and blast everything in range. The CT's, theoretically at least, would be caught between us in a deadly squeeze.

Frankly, I didn't see it. I mean, considering that, as I understood it, the strength of the CT's was never put at more than a couple hundred, the size of the operation made no sense to me. But ours not to reason why.

I was beginning to feel ill again. I had moments of dizziness and nausea. I was losing weight, when I barely had an ounce to spare. The fever, too, had returned. But I said nothing. This wasn't heroics; goodness knows there wasn't enough action up there to create heroes anyway. I suppose it was stupid pride, in a way. A reluctance to fall when so many others were standing.

We set out then on our long march, scheduled to last several weeks. After seventy-two hours of hacking our way through a rain forest without seeing a sign of any CT, we set up camp and began clearing an area for a helicopter landing pad. Backbreaking work, this. The ironwood trees in the forest were aptly named indeed. My physical condition was now steadily and rapidly declining. I was exhausted. By fortunate coincidence, I collapsed the day the helicopter pad was completed. I was evacuated on the first chopper to arrive.

I was comatose for the better part of a month, slipping in and out of consciousness, in and out of delirium, my feverish dreams filled with lunatic collages of galloping horses, naked women, Atty Persse, Aunt Ida and steak and kidney pie—all in brilliant Technicolor. I knew, vaguely, that I was in a hospital somewhere, and that I was filled with tubes and needles. For a time I was in any oxygen tent.

When I came out of it, a nurse told me I was at Kinrara Hospital in Kuala Lumpur. I was down with malaria and pneumonia, a deadly combination. But she assured me that the worst was over, the doctors had it under control. However, I would require an extended period of convalescence at the hospital.

"How long?" I asked.

She wasn't sure. "Perhaps six months. You're very weak. We'll have to build you up."

I closed my eyes and drifted back into a peaceful sleep. Six months in Kuala Lumput couldn't be bad. All those lovely nurses.

As I recovered, slowly but surely, regaining my strength and putting on weight, I resumed my old ways. I made a few extra Malay dollars running errands. I sneaked out to the race track at Bukit Timah and won a few more. I took up with one particularly beautiful Malay named Tan. Her father was a prosperous merchant in Kuala Lumpur. He didn't approve of me at all, but Tan and I really had a thing for each other. When I was well enough to get some leave from the hospital I moved in with her, and for the rest of my stay in Malay we virtually but not virtuously lived together.

When I was due to return home I asked her to come back with me, to marry me. But she had more sense than I did, perhaps. She realised that a romance between a

British soldier and a Malay, high class though she might be, was one thing in Kuala Lumpur, but a horse of quite another colour in England.

I had been in hospital some four months or so, pretty much coming and going as I pleased, when one day a nurse told me that there was a Signals major there to see me. Arrangements had been made for me to meet him in the office of the hospital's commanding officer. I wondered what this was all about. Hardly good news. My last meeting with a major had been the disaster at Singapore.

I entered the C.O.'s office, stood to attention and saluted. The major told me to stand at ease, then, to my amazement, offered me his hand in greeting. "Payne," he said, "I heard you were here and I wanted to meet you." A twinkle came into his eye. "Know why?"

"Haven't a clue, Sir."

"You remember a horse named The Mallard?"

"The Mallard! That rotten beast really savaged me one day. At Newbury. Turned on me in his box and bit me. Nearly did me a permanent injury. But how do you know about me and The Mallard, sir?"

The major laughed. "I recently bought him. He's stabled here at Lumpur. I got the whole story about you from the chief of police in my district. Apparently his sister works as a hairdresser in a shop in Winchester you mother goes to. Your mother sent word through to him to keep an eye out for you. He's a regular punter, this chap, and remembered reading in *The Sporting Life* or somewhere about you and The Mallard. So when I bought him, and your mother sent the word along you were in Kinrara, I thought I'd come by and meet you."

I shook my head in wonderment. "Small world," I said.

"Indeed," he agreed. "And what do you think of my buying The Mallard?"

"If the major will excuse me, sir, I think the major's

crazy. That's a bad horse, sir."

"Yes . . . well." He stood up and shook my hand again. "Come and see me soon, Payne. There's a chap I'd like you to meet. We can talk about racing and all that." He told me where I could find him, and said he'd arranged with the hospital C.O. for me to have a pass on weekends, when there was racing at Bukit Timah.

I went out to the major's that next weekned. He was truly a nice guy who was able to put aside his rank and forget about the Army when we got together. We had an expertise and a love of horse racing in common, and that was good enough for him. He introduced me, that weekend, to a very strange and mysterious man who was to havc a profound influence on my life many years later, when I began training horses on my own. He was small and slim, dark-complexioned, perhaps thirty-five years old. He spoke with an accent. I couldn't figure out if he was Egyptian, Filipino, Singalese or what. I knew him only as "Georgie". If out of curiosity I tried to find out more about him a veil came down over his dark eyes and he clammed up.

Georgie was a vet. He seemed to be able to work miracles with animals to make them rise practically from the dead. He said to me once, "Men are such fools. They throw away so much that is useful because they are lazy or ignorant." I remember once he took a whole string of sick mules the Army was about to destroy and fixed them up as good as new.

But Georgie specialized in fixing up race horses. That's what he did for the major, who had several in his stables Kuala Lumpur. I was under the impression that he also did quite a bit of the same in Australia; he was continually flying back and forth, and was friendly with several Australian jockeys riding in Malaya at the time. Bill Williamson was one of them and another lad named Parnell.

I watched Georgie make a winner out of The Mallard. First he gelded him, which removed the savagery in the big stallion, then gave him a series of treatments that to me proved an eye-opener. He brewed a mixture of foul-smelling herbs, mixed it with The Mallard's feed, then followed up with a series of injections.

"Vitamins," he told me. "Not dope. Vitamins." I was more than a bit sceptical then, but in later years my own experiences led me to believe that Georgie was using steroids and vitamin B-12 in combination, not only on The Mallard, but on all the horses he tended. In any case, I saw the effects of the treatment. The Mallard won first time out, ridden by a Chinese jockey. But I also noticed that Georgie's treatments did not have a lasting effect. He could get a horse "up" for a race, but a week or so later the animal reverted to its form, whatever it might have been before the injections.

What I saw, what I learned, I filed away in the back of my mind. My time in Malaya was coming to an end. I was to be invalided back home. And, of course, my only thought was to get back into racing as soon as I could.

Almost two years had passed since I'd said goodbye to Bob Read and Atty Persse. Times had changed. I had changed. I'd grown a few inches, put on weight. When I went up to Lambourn to see Bob he rubbed his jaw thoughtfully. "You might try your hand at steeple-chasing, Duke. But you're too big to ride on the flat."

I asked about a job at the yard, as a stable lad, but Bob, obviously embarrassed, told me the way it was. "Duke, nobody can afford to pay you the adult rate of eight quid a week when they can still get an apprentice to do the same job for five bob."

Recognising the truth in what he said did nothing to blunt the sharp edge of my disappointment. What in hell was I going to do now? Was I finished in racing forever? I didn't see myself as a steeplechase jockey, even if I was willing to go back to square one at some other trainer's yard. Neither did I want to go back to Bassett Green. I remained at Lambourn, sleeping where I could find a bed, hoping something would turn up.

One night Joe Mercer took me to a dance at Newbury to help cheer me up. I met a girl there and, neither for the first time nor the last, a girl helped me in a time of trouble. I told her a bit about my problems.

"Duke," she said, "why don't you come around and stay at our house for a few days? Dad's a bit of a racing fan and I'm sure he won't mind. Just till you find something."

I was grateful enough for any favours. I went home with her after the dance and, sure enough, her parents were willing to give me the settee for a few days. They trusted me, and though I never claim to be an angel, I don't betray a trust. I didn't go near their daughter's bedroom.

Came the weekend, and the man approached me, "Say, Duke, if you're needing a bit of money, I'm short a man this weekend. Want to give me a hand?"

"Sure," I said. "Doing what?"

"Cleaning windows. That's the business I'm in."

I shrugged. "Cleaning windows can't be any harder than cleaning out a horse box."

It was lots easier, I found. I worked like a demon that weekend, much faster and more efficiently than some of the other lads on the man's crew. We cleaned the windows of a new block of council flats, hundreds of windows, in preparation for the new tenants' arrival.

On Sunday night, back at the man's house, he smiled approvingly. "That was a grand job of work you did, Duke."

"Glad I could help out," I said. "How much did I earn."

"Thirty quid."

"Thirty pounds!" You could have knocked me over with a feather. "Thirty pounds for that?"

"Yup. It's a good business, Duke. You earned it and here it is." He counted out the notes into my hand.

Monday morning bright and early I was on my way up to Hursley to see my Aunt Sue and Uncle Fred. I borrowed forty pounds from them, bought an extension ladder and bucket in the village of Chandler's Ford nearby and began walking along the Hursley Road, ladder on shoulder, bucket in hand, knocking on doors.

"Any windows need washing? One and six the front, three and six all around."

I was in business. Duke Payne, window cleaner. "Window" Payne, they called me, and I cleaned up a fortune.

CHAPTER FIVE

I MADE OUT like a bandit.

At the second house I went to a little grey-haired old lady answered the door. Yes, she could do with having her windows cleaned. All around. When I'd finished the job she asked me in for a cup of tea. "What's you name, son?" she asked.

"Ken Payne."

"Payne? You related to Alfred and Lily Payne from Bassett Green?"

"That's my Mum and Dad."

She smiled sweetly. "Then you've been here before, son."

"Me? Never."

"You wouldn't remember, of course. You were just little. It was during the war, during the Blitz. I remember it like it was yesterday. There was a big raid on Southampton. Your Dad was trapped on the docks and couldn't get home. There were no lorries, so your Mum walked here all the way from Bassett Green, with you and your crippled sister in a push chair. Then, when the bombs started falling here, you hid right under this very table till it was all over." She laughed. "What a dear little lad you were."

The revival of the old wartime memory gave me half the houses in Chandler's Ford by the time the week was out. The old lady brought me into her neighbour's house where they swapped stories about the Blitz while I cleaned the windows—and so on, from neighbour to neighbour. I made about fifteen pounds in that first week, not bad at all for 1957.

Bit by bit, month by month, I built a business. I expanded my route to cover Chilworth, a classy area where the ladies of the house wouldn't let me leave my ladder and bucket overnight, as they did in Chandler's Ford. So I made a deal there with a petrol station manager; I'd do his windows in exchange for storage of my equipment. Each night when I finished my rounds I returned either to Bassett Green or to my aunt and uncle in Hursley, depending on where I'd been working.

I didn't forget about horse racing. But I had to earn a living. I read the sporting papers and followed events, bet a pound here and there on a horse. One day, reading *Sporting Life*, I spotted a good one. She was a two-year-old maiden filly named Twin Tegge, out of Bob Read's yard. An itch told me Bob was pulling off one of his little coups. I put fifty pounds on her at 4–1, and she won it easily. I now had two hundred and fifty pounds in the kitty. I bought an old Ford Popular van with a roof rack, another ladder and bucket and hired myself a lad.

I hustled, I can vouch for that. You have to if you want to make a success of window cleaning, because there are always good reasons available for not working. The weather turns bad, nobody's home when you call, or the lady is short of housekeeping money and tells you to skip this week. But I worked hard and discovered that people were very nice to me. As time went by I was able to add more vans and more lads, and was building a window-cleaning business that stretched from the River Itchen west to the Avon, from the New Forest north to Salisbury and Winchester.

Soon enough I found out that a lot of those jokes they tell about window cleaners are true. It's incredible what some women will get up to, and how direct they can be. More than one housewife would invite me in for a cup of tea at ten in the morning and serve it wearing a transparent nightie with nothing underneath, or accidentally on purpose let a loose robe flap open to reveal the tantalising pink flesh.

I was hardly reluctant, just repeatedly amazed. I took what was offered without conscience, and, I suppose, put the horns on a great many husbands from The Solent to the Vale of Pewsey. This is not stated with any great degree of pride or arrogance. I was no Casanova, just young and fit and not ugly; many people said in those days that I looked a lot like Tommy Steele.

A number of strange situations developed. I'll never forget a certain attractive older woman who lived in a big house near Salisbury. We were entwined on the sofa as usual one afternoon, while my ladder stood idle at the back of the house, when in the middle of the proceedings she suddenly disentangled herself and switched on the television. My ego wasn't the only object that quickly wilted.

But she returned to me and we picked up the rhythm without missing a beat. I paid no attention to the TV, which seemed to be showing some outside broadcast involving the Royal Family and sundry dignitaries. Our ardour grew, she became ever more impassioned and then finally with a great cry she crumpled in my arms. After a moment she sighed with deep satisfaction. "Marvellous," she said. "I swore I'd do that while the bastard was getting his medal." Sweet revenge, as it were, on her husband, who was getting his just desserts in two places at once for being a giant of industry.

For some of these lonely and embittered housewives, a simple cuckolding job on their husbands wasn't enough. They needed romance. Which meant that the green-eyed monster of jealousy reared its ugly head. For business reasons, therefore, if nothing else, I had to be discreet, and I had to be strong—if my meaning is clear.

There was one new luxury-housing development in the New Forest that truly gave me a bad time. When the first house was built and occupied, the builders tipped me off (I had this arrangement with builders, for a fee of course). I went around to see the little lady of the house, who turned out to be a stunning brunette. In short order, we had a thing going.

Then the second house was completed. A lovely blonde moved in. As it happened, the brunette worked afternoons so I was able to service her mornings, front and back (windows as well) and give the blonde a good going over in the afternoon.

Came the completion of the third house and I begged the builders (who knew what was going on) to have compassion on me and find a couple of old-age pensioners for it. When I next called at the site, I kept my fingers crossed. A few minutes later I was up a ladder, actually cleaning the windows of house number one when I heard a female voice calling to me from below. I looked down and groaned inwardly. It was no pensioner, but another blonde, a rather buxom lady with an incredible set of boobs almost falling out of a scooped-neck blouse. From my vantage point on the ladder it was like looking down into the Cheddar Gorge.

"I saw your van," she cooed. "Would you come 'round to number three when you're finished?"

I gave the windows at number one a rather less professional rub than I did the lady of the house, then hurried off to number three, hoping the buxom blonde was either faithful or frigid—preferably both, just to make sure. Without further ceremony I parked my ladder against the house and went to work. When I got to what was obviously the lady's bedroom window I could see displayed on the ledge inside several framed photos of her—all nudes. She came through the bedroom doorway then, apparently fresh from the bath, a brief wrapper tied loosely around her body. With those boobs of hers, you might as well have tried to hide an elephant under a postage stamp.

She smiled at me, came to the windows, opened one. "Do you like them?" she said, pointing to the nude photos. I was doomed once again.

There were times in those early years of my business when I felt like a trained seal, thrown a fish for a virtuoso performance. There were other moments when I felt like a stallion in stud. The difference was merely a matter of money, I blush to admit. For there were those days when I solved a problem of cash flow in the business by a visit to one of my wealthier regulars. I never asked for money, I never discussed business problems with any of my women, but somehow they knew I was struggling, and somehow they even knew, and accepted, that I was using them. Perhaps they felt it was fair enough, quid pro quo—if you'll pardon the pun: they were using me, too. In any case, there were several big houses I could go to, dally for an hour or two, and find an envelope with fifty pounds or so in it waiting for me in the hallway when I left, or stuck in my jacket pocket.

There was yet another way I used women in my business. When I began to spread my wings and go after industrial window-cleaning contracts, I often found I couldn't get past the guard at the factory gates, or obtain an interview with an office manager. I hired a couple of models as salesgirls, dolled them up in short skirts and tight jumpers, and had no more trouble with gate-guards and bumptious clerks.

It was during this interval that I met Ann, who was to become my first wife. At the time I was living like a gypsy, pretty much sleeping wherever it was I could hang my hat that night. I also had a caravan parked illegally in the New Forest to which I could repair if nothing better offered itself. But most weekends I preferred to stay with my family in Bassett Green. I was there one Saturday night when my sister Sonja came in with a girl in her mid-twenties, a pretty girl with a complexion like an English rose. She was slim, petite, demure.

Sonja introduced the girl as Ann Lovell, a co-worker at the office. She said they'd been to a dance, and now Ann had missed the last bus back to her home in Calemoor, in the New Forest. Would I mind giving her a lift in my van? I didn't mind at all.

We didn't talk much during the drive; the usual chit-chat: what did I do, what did she do, a bit about my service in Malaya and so forth. Although it was late by the time we got to her house, she invited me in for a cup of tea. Her father was still up and we were introduced. It was instant dislike. We rubbed each other the wrong way at once and events later on only aggravated the irritation.

Mr. Lovell didn't like my looks, the way I wore my hair a bit long, the way I talked. He was a red-hot radical, too, so most of all he railed against my soldiering in Malaya. He considered the CT's to be not terrorists at all but poor peasants fighting for liberation from centuries of colonial exploitation. Well, true enough, even today one man's terrorist is another man's freedom fighter. Having seen conditions in Malaya I might even have been prepared to concede him half a point. But I resented his attitude, which seemed to hold me personally responsible for all the starving children and downtrodden farmers in Malaya.

What really put me off him was his relationship with Ann's kid sister, Heather. She was only seven, and when we met for the first time she said to me, "Hello, I'm Heather. I was a mistake."

Mr. Lovell was a man of about fifty then, his wife not much younger, and obviously Heather was a late child; a mistake. But to let the poor kid know it? It seemed to me Mr. Lovell treated Heather as though she was a nuisance, like one of the neighbour's kids who came around the house too often and couldn't be got rid of. She was a sweet kid, too, Heather. I felt sorry for her.

Looking back on it all, I can forgive the man. Hindsight makes us all divine, I suppose. He was wasting away with tuberculosis, even then a dying man. And he knew it. No doubt he was embittered by his illness and now a lifetime of repressed frustrations—don't we all have them?—must have risen like bile in his throat, choking him, along with the phlegm from his consumptive lungs.

But at the time Mr. Lovell was not my favourite person. Still, I dated Ann regularly, both of us ignoring his outspoken distaste for me. We had good times together. We went dancing, or to the pictures or sometimes simply out for a meal and a drive in the van. During the summer months one of our favourite things was a swim at secluded Kimmeridge Bay. My collie, Amber, went just about everywhere with us.

Ann was a religious person, though not a churchgoer. She had deep convictions, however. She was a virgin, and I respected her wish to remain one. I wanted her, but my sexual desires had more than enough substitute outlets. I liked Ann, I cared for her, but not so deeply that I would give up all my other women and don a hair shirt.

We went on this way for about a year. Then, suddenly, she seemed to cool. Either she avoided me or acted strangely when she was with me. One night, finally, I telephoned her and was told by her father she wouldn't talk to me. I decided it was time for a showdown. I drove over in the van and demanded to know what was wrong.

"Not here, Ken," she said. "Let's go for a drive."

We drove for a long time in utter silence. When we came to the New Forest I pulled off the road some hundred yards and parked. I shut off the motor, turned to her. "Okay, Ann," I said, "now tell me what's with you? I mean if you want to give me the elbow, that's all right, just say so. But I don't like this silent treatment and I think I deserve better than that from you."

I had hardly finished my little speech before she burst into tears. She put her head on my chest. "Oh Ken," she said, sobbing miserably. "Oh Ken . . ."

"Hey, hey," I said, shaken, surprised. I stroked her hair. "Hey, whatever it is, it can't be that bad. What is it, Ann, something I've done? Your father, or what?"

She raised her head, sniffed, took a deep breath, brushed away tears. "Ken, I'm ill," she said. Tears came again, in a gush. "Ken, I think I'm going to die, Ken!"

"What are you talking about?" I said. "What do you mean?"

"It's true." I could see she was trying to gain control of herself, taking in deep gulps of air, her breathing heavy. I waited, just holding her, stroking her, soothing her. After a few moments she began to breathe normally. She took a handkerchief from her purse, wiped her eyes, blew her nose.

"Tell me about it," I said quietly.

"Well, you know, Ken, I think I told you, because of my father, because of his tuberculosis, all of us have been going to hospital for a long time, having regular check-ups and things. X-rays and that. I think everybody has to do that if somebody with bad tuberculosis is living at home."

"You mean because it might be catching?" I interrupted.

"That's right. Well, a couple of weeks ago they told me at hospital that I . . . that I had a patch on my lung, Ken." She began to shake and cry softly.

"So what does that mean?" I protested. "That doesn't mean anything."

She nodded. "It does, Ken. I . . . I already quit my job. Next week I have to go into sanitorium for treatment."

I sat there for long moments, staring through the windscreen into the soft summer darkness, feeling awfully inadequate. I said to her then, "But how serious is it? I mean, really, Ann? Nowadays nobody dies of tuberculosis. Your father got it ages ago, before the war, when they didn't know how to treat these things."

"That's just it," she said. "My father. Ken, I've been watching him waste away into a skeleton all these years. I'm afraid that'll happen to me, Ken, I'm really afraid!"

What could I say to her? I don't know what I said to her that night, but I talked, talked, droned on and on, comforted her, told her things I didn't know about, didn't believe. Anything to stem the flow of tears, to calm her fears.

We held on to each other there in the darkness of the New Forest, held on in an embrace warmed by a new need. It was a gorgeous night, with no moon but lots of stars. Hardly a sound disturbed the stillness. A young owl squawked and was answered by a hoot from its mother. Now and again a car would pass on the distant road, light beams stabbing into the darkness, motor purring.

"Make love to me, Ken," she said.

"Pardon?"

"Make love to me. You do want to, don't you?"

"But Ann . . ."

She smiled. "I know. I'm a virgin. Men always make more of a fuss over that than a woman. I want you to make love to me, Ken."

"Ann, you're only saying that because of this thing with the sanitorium."

"All right, suppose I am, Ken?" She was in control of herself now, assured, determined, reconciled. "Why shouldn't I, then? Who knows how long I'll be in that place? It might be years. I might . . . I might never come out, or be a dried up old lady by the time I do. Please, Ken, don't make me keep asking."

We left the van then. I took an old blanket out of the back and spread it on the ground. We lay down together. I didn't hurry. I tried to prepare her for it, get her turned on to it. She clung to me, her arms around my neck, trusting me, her cheek wet with tears against mine.

Later, when I drove her home again, I promised her I'd visit her regularly in the sanitorium, she could depend on it. I told her not to worry. I was sure she wouldn't be in there very long. But in fact she was there three years.

I kept my word to Ann about the visits. The sanitorium was nearby in Chandler's Ford, and so it was no trouble at all for me to dash over there a couple of times a week and on a Sunday. As time went on she grew to need me more and more and I—well, perhaps my need was to be needed. In any case, with the passing months, with the years, a link was forged between us, a link that I came to realise was really a chain binding me to her. I wasn't sure that's what I wanted, but I was powerless to break it.

Meantime, Kenneth Payne Cleaning Limited grew to giant proportions. At its peak in the early 1960's it employed nearly 700 people. It was ticking over nicely, almost running itself, enabling me to spend more time at the race tracks. I renewed old friendships. I became a regular at Bob Read's yard, just popping in for a coffee and a chat and to look over the horseflesh. Bob had married a wealthy woman, and a wonderful marriage it was too, for both of them. With money behind him, Bob had been able to buy first-class yearlings at the sales, and his yard had changed completely. Gone were the ragbag platers and ageing donkeys. Bob had first-class horses which were winning first-class races, proving what I had always said about Bob: he was a brilliant trainer.

I was particularly friendly with Wilfred Walker, who was Bob's travelling head lad. Will would never give me an outright tip on a horse; but he would say to me, as we'd walk by one of the boxes, "Now there's a fine filly, Duke. At seven furlongs with no more'n eight stone on her she can't be beat. Especially on soft ground." He would tell me things like that. I'd watch the form and the entries and when I saw where Will's information would pay off I'd make my bet.

I won some tidy sums that way, a bundle one year alone on Done Me and Phony Flower.

Toward the end of Ann's second year at the sanitorium she developed diabetes. Her father blamed this complication on side effects from a new, experimental anti-tubercular drug she'd been receiving. He also blamed me for allowing her to be treated, as he termed it, "like a bloody guinea-pig". As though I had any power to affect her treatments at all. Whether or not the new drugs were in fact to blame is a moot point; I know there was some controversy about them at the time.

Fortunately, the diabetes was quickly brought under control. Ann was in no mortal danger; she was frail, but definitely on the road to recovery. Although she would need to be careful of strain and overwork, she would be able to cope with an office job. When she realised that she would soon be released from the sanitorium, Ann said to me, "We will be married when I get out of here, won't we, Ken?"

I suppose I shouldn't have been surprised at the question; perhaps I had given Ann every reason to believe that marriage would be the inevitable outcome of our relationship. I hesitated for a moment before answering and she said, quickly, "You don't have to, you know."

But I did have to. I couldn't let her down now, after her suffering, with the illness still a part of her, with her need for me so obvious. I wasn't in love with her, whatever that overabused word "love" means. I don't know, maybe sympathy and a willingness to accept the burden of being needed is a kind of love.

"Of course we'll get married," I assured her. "Don't be silly. It was just that for a second there I panicked." I laughed nervously. "Every prospective bridegroom does that."

She smiled, and her pale face came alive, and she began to speak of making a home and where we would live and whether or not she'd be strong enough to have kids. I hardly absorbed a word. I didn't want to marry anybody. Not just then.

I told my parents, and my aunts and uncles. They all liked Ann, but understandably were concerned about her health, and the possibility that I'd be bound to an invalid. One Sunday, when I was having dinner at my Aunt Sue's in Hursley, she told me that Viscount Lifford wanted to see me at his house.

Lord Lifford greeted me warmly, as he always did, and asked me how the business was going. He poured a sherry for each of us, then said, "Ken (he never called me Duke) I understand you and that nice girl of yours are going to be married when she comes out of hospital."

"Yes, that's right, sir." I assumed my aunt had told him.

"Where are you going to live?"

"I don't know. I hadn't given it too much thought. I have that caravan in the Forest."

"A caravan! My boy, you can't take a girl out of a tuberculosis sanitorium and put her in a caravan. I'll tell you what I'm going to do. I'm going to sell you one of my cottages."

I laughed, without humour. "That's very kind of you, sir," I said. "But I couldn't possibly afford to buy a cottage. The business is going well, but it all seems to go out as fast as it comes in. I don't have any money saved. I don't think I could even raise a mortgage."

Lord Lifford stroked his moustache, a magnificent specimen of growth. He looked very much like Jimmy Edwardes, the comedian; portly, jolly, ruddy-complexioned. After a while he said, "Tell you what, Ken. Can you raise three hundred pounds?"

"Three hundred? Yes. I can get three hundred together. Why, sir?"

"Never mind. Just get it, and you be at your aunt's solicitor's on Tuesday morning with your cheque book."

On Tuesday morning I went around there, and old Mr. Yates said to me, "Kenneth, write a cheque for three hundred and twenty-four pounds."

"All right," I said. "But what for?"

Mr. Yates looked at me over the top of his spectacles. Kingly old Mr. Yates needed only a tall stool and a quill pen to complete the picture he made of the Dickensian solicitor. "Lord Lifford," he said, "for reasons unbeknowst to any but his kind self, is conveying to you two cottages, one with vacant possession, the other with sitting tenant, inclusive of four acres of land, with freehold thereon, for the sum of three hundred and twenty-four pounds." He pointed a tremulous finger at me. "It's worth ten times that, and more."

"I know," I said, hardly daring to believe my good luck. "I don't understand it. Are you sure it's all right?"

"Of course it's all right. Write the cheque, Kenneth, write the cheque before Lord Lifford comes to his senses and withdraws the offer."

That's how I obtained the bargain of the century. An incredible man, Lord Lifford. I owe him so much and it is because of him, and others like him who treated me so kindly when I needed help, that today I have such nightmares of regret; the cataclysm that shattered my life in 1976 sent tremors in all directions, and I feel that I let so many people down, betrayed them.

This veritable gift from Lord Lifford began a new phase in my life. It got me back into the world of horse racing. I thought then that I had the whole world at my fingertips. Just as well none of us can see much past our own noses, or we'd be too frightened to try anything at all.

CHAPTER SIX

"KEN, you got any use for some good timber?"

Sunday dinner at Bassett Green, my Dad talking to me between mouthfuls of roast.

"I suppose I could use some, yes," I said to him. "Been thinking about building a couple of loose boxes, actually. Be nice to have a horse, just for riding. And one for Ann, too, when we get married and she's strong enough to ride."

My Dad nodded. "Tell you what, then. I can get you some terrific stuff, on the cheap. All good tongue-and-groove board. Enough to build all the boxes you'd want."

"Where from?"

"The Navy. They're selling a couple of minesweepers to the Indian Navy, and they got all this board they used for cocooning them after the war to keep 'em from rusting. For thirty or forty quid I can get you a trailer load."

"Okay, Dad, you're on."

With the help of my Dad, and a couple of his friends on the docks, I arranged to rent a trailer, and we got the timber over to my land on Lord Lifford's estate. On weekends they'd all come over and we'd get to work building. My Dad, who'd been a proper shipwright before the war, knew his way around good timber, and in a month's time I had two sweet boxes ready. All I needed now were horses. And then along came Fate at the gallop.

I was up a ladder, cleaning windows for Mrs. Gwen Southwell, when it began. I heard a whinnying first, then the clatter of hooves on cobbles, and a girl's voice shouting. I turned, looked down, and there came a beautiful little chestnut charging past my ladder, eyes wild, saliva dripping, tail twitching. Then I saw Jane Southwell come limping into view, her riding habit covered with leaves and dirt, her riding cap gone. Jane was Mrs. Southwell's 15-year-old daughter, and obviously she'd just had a bad time with her horse.

She saw me on the ladder and called out, "Can you help me, Ken?"

I climbed down. "Sure. You stay here. That horse is in no mood to be played with. I'll let her calm down a bit and lead her back. Throw you, did she?"

"Yes. And not for the first time. She doesn't seem to like me very much."

"What's her name?"

"Fantasia."

By now Mrs. Southwell had joined us, having heard the noise.

"I told Jane not to ride that filly anymore," she said to me. "There's something wrong with her."

The name Fantasia suddenly rang a bell with me. "Did you get her from Charlie Pratt at Lambourn?"

"That's right. Why, do you know the horse, Kenneth?"

"Yeah, I think I do. Tommy Lipton bred her. But she's bred for racing, Mrs. Southwell. No wonder Jane can't ride her. Needs a stronger hand than Jane could ever give her. How'd you come to buy a racehorse for Jane to ride?"

"Charlie sold her to me because she wasn't good enough for racing. She's too small, barely fifteen hands. I thought she'd be all right for Jane. Obviously I was wrong."

"Well, you'd better sell her off, Mrs. Southwell, before

your girl gets hurt."

"Why don't you take her, Kenneth?"

"Me? I've got no use for her, Mrs. Southwell. I couldn't afford to buy and keep a horse like that just for the fun of it."

"I'm not asking you to buy her, just take her. I want Fantasia to be well taken care of and I know you can do it. I'll pay you for board and feed until I find a proper owner for her."

That's how I came to train my first horse. Or, at least, have one in a box alongside my cottage. At the time I took her off Mrs. Southwell's hands I entertained no thoughts about training Fantasia for anything at all.

I worked like a beaver in those days, trying to earn money, hoping to build up a bank balance so that when Ann got out of the hospital and we got married there'd be a few quid behind us to get started. But no matter what I did, no matter what I earned, it all seemed to vanish as fast as it came in.

The window-cleaning business was bringing in money. But considering the size of the business and my turnover I wasn't making enough. Not to live the way I wanted to live. So I expanded into pigs. It seemed like a good business. I'd met a few pig farmers and they seemed prosperous enough to me. So I got some pig pens built and for £45 each bought eight sows "in pig" from a farmer in Whitechurch. When I'd get a litter I'd go over to Salisbury market and sell the piglets for about eight pounds each. With ten or twelve pigs to a litter, I was making a reasonable profit. Feeding them wasn't costing me much. I'd go around to council estates and hotels collecting swill for them.

I don't know how I did it all. I was working seven days a week, what with cleaning windows, running the business, feeding the pigs, looking after Fantasia and visiting Ann at the hospital. And yet I added a little chicken run. I guess maybe I just liked the atmosphere of a little farmyard, with the smell of the animals and the sounds of the pigs and the chickens. I wasn't the only one who liked it. Fantasia liked it, too. She seemed content, calm, happy to have the chickens strutting in and out of her box, pecking away at the ground, flapping about. When I'd take her out in the misty dawn she'd gallop gracefully around the estate, responding to my touch, never giving me a moment's trouble. I was beginning to hope that Mrs. Southwell would not soon find an owner for her.

At Salisbury one day, selling off some piglets, I met Ralph Emery, who had a big pig farm at Romsey, in the New Forest. We fell to talking about pigs and farms and animals in general, and soon discovered that we had a shared interest in horses. Ralph, in fact, owned a few ponies and raced them regularly at Hawthorn Hill in the New Forest.

"Maybe you'd like to ride one of 'em some Saturday night," Ralph offered, when he learned I'd been apprenticed to Atty Persse.

"I don't think I ought to, thanks just the same," I said. "I've been thinking I might try to ride steeplechase one day, Ralph, and if the Jockey Club ever found out I'd been riding at a flapping track like Hawthorn they'd never give me a licence."

But I invited Ralph over to have a look at Fantasia, and when he saw her he was clearly impressed. "That's a good looking filly you got there, Ken. Would you take her out on the gallops now and again with one of mine?"

"Sure, why not?" I said. "Where do you gallop your ponies?"

"Chattis Hill. Vernon Cross lets me use his gallops."

I knew Vernon. He was a good trainer. So the following Saturday Ralph sent his trailer around for me and Fantasia, and he brought along a pony he had named Twig, and we went over to Stockbridge to the gallops.

Twig was a beautiful little filly, a true thoroughbred, not a half or three-quarter bred like most of the other ponies that raced at Hawthorn. Ralph had bought her at Ascot sales from one of the Rothschild family because she was too small to race on the regular tracks. But she beat everything she raced against at Hawthorn.

Yet she couldn't beat Fantasia. Ralphs's eyes popped open when he saw what I could do on that filly on the gallops. At four furlongs, even four and a half, Fantasia was the fastest thing on four legs. But she faded after that. She just didn't have the stamina, which was why she'd been sold down to Mrs. Southwell in the first place. But as a horse to run against on the gallops, she was first rate.

One day, in fact, Vernon Cross put one of his good horses, Brown Top, against Twig and Fantasia. I wasn't up on Fantasia that day; I'd brought along a jockey named Roy Nelson for a ride. The three horses broke evenly but in a couple of strides Fantasia was out in front. I knew she'd break out there, she was a real front runner and didn't like to see any other animal ahead of her. She was way out, light lengths in front, at three furlongs, five lengths out at four furlongs, then the other two caught her and passed her.

Still, she impressed Vernon Cross. "That's a filly I'd like to own," he said. "I've never seen such speed."

"But she'll never win a race unless they shorten one to four furlongs," I volunteered. "She almost stops short at the marker."

He nodded his head. "Still, I wouldn't mind giving her a try."

I imparted this information to Mrs. Southwell, but she was having none of it. "I don't want her racing, Kenneth. Gallop her all you want, but until I find an owner for her, no racing."

So I kept Fantasia on the gallops, running her regularly with Twig. Ralph had plans to take Twig up to Wales for a big pony race at Prestatyn. I had intended to go along, but Ann told me she was due to be released from the sanatorium on that same day. I gave Ralph twenty pounds to bet for me on Twig—she won—and remained behind to be with Ann.

I picked her up at the sanatorium and took her to her parents' house. Our plans were for her to remain there for a few months while I fixed up the cottage and made arrangements for the wedding. I still had doubts, forebodings, about this marriage, but there was no way I saw that I could back out without breaking Ann's heart and, perhaps, causing her to relapse into ill health.

If my heart wasn't in it, certainly I put my back into it. I got to work cleaning up the cottage, buying new furniture, getting curtains made, rugs put down, pipes laid for modern plumbing. I borrowed from the bank up to my ears to buy the furniture and kitchen appliances. I wanted Ann to have the best, and I wanted her to be happy.

One fine summer's day in 1961, we were married at the Netley Marsh Church in the New Forest.

Sad to say, I don't suppose we spent a truly happy day together from that moment to the bitter end of our unfortunate marriage.

We got married for all the wrong reasons. We were hopelessly incompatible. Ann is long dead now, and I have no reason or desire to sully her memory. For another kind of man she would have made a wonderful wife, just as I, for the right reasons, with the right woman, could have made a good husband.

Some women marry a man for what he is; others for what they believe they can make of him after they marry him. Ann married a wild window-cleaner who loved horses and animals of all kinds, who did not work by a clock, who was gregarious and believed in living life to the fullest.

Ann wanted a husband who worked regular hours, preferably at something other than window-cleaning, which she thought demeaning. Not that she was a snob; she thought I should become a milkman or a postman or something of the sort, or take a job in an office. She was an excellent cook and housekeeper, neat to the point of being fastidious, which can become a problem when you keep pigs and chickens and a horse within just four acres of ground. She hated the animals; hated the noise and the dirt and the smells.

Her parents were no help at all. Her father was at me all the time to give up my business. My interest in horses irritated him even more. He was such a militant Left-wing socialist that he despised on principle all the people I knew on the big estates, including Lord Lifford, who had been so kind and generous to me and Ann regarding the cottage and land. And because he despised them, he despised me by association.

We were also sexually incompatible. Ann was repressed, partly because she wanted no children—another sore point between us. I loved kids and wanted two or three. So sex for us was an infrequent and mechanical contact. Again, I wish to make it clear that I am not carping. Merely offering an explanation for the utter failure of our marriage. I was hardly an angel, I'm sure. Perhaps I could have done more to compromise, perhaps I could have been more patient with Ann, helped her sexually with my own experience in that area, or suggested we seek counselling. Perhaps, if I had cared more, I might have given it all up and become a milkman. But we are basically what we are, and I can't honestly believe that Ken Payne in a new suit of clothes would have been anything else than Ken Payne underneath. Any more than putting overalls on Ann and getting her to muck out a stable once or twice would have changed her.

All too soon after our wedding day we were left with nothing but the façade of a marriage. We sent through the motions, politely, rarely arguing, perhaps each in our own way hoping that something would happen to alter the circumstances. Or even more likely, thinking back on it, each of us paralysed by inertia, unable to do more than drift along in a relationship that was not good enough to enjoy, yet not quite bad enough to force either of us to call it quits. At least, not at that point.

Many a night I went to my Aunt Ida's pub, The Cuckoo, seeking the warmth of companionship, of conversation. Often I'd sit in a corner with old Paddy Baldwin, and over a few beers we'd swap stories, talk horses. Old Paddy, nearly seventy then, who was to turn around Neronton for me a few years later, had more stories to tell than anybody else I ever knew. I think he made up half of them, but since they were always the best ones, I never showed my suspicions that they were born in Paddy's fertile imagination.

One night I told Paddy about Georgie, the strange vet I'd met out in Malaya, and described his treatment of horses. Paddy was all ears; he was fascinated. As stud groom to Lady Bouverie he, of course, had a keen interest in the training and care of horses.

"Kenny," he said to me, "I've got a gelding named Three Gates I'd like to try that on."

I was a bit dubious. "You want to win a race with him?"

"Good Lord, no," said Paddy. "Three Gates isn't going to race anymore. He's lost all interest since they've gelded him. But that ain't no reason why I can't get him fit. He's so listless right now I can't even get him to gallop. Gelding a horse does it to 'em like that sometimes."

It was agreed then between us that we'd get in touch with certain persons in Australia who could supply us with what we needed; Georgie had given me all the necessary information in Kuala Lumpur. I wrote to Australia, and in the ensuing weeks the letters and money went over there as requested. It cost about fifty pounds for the instructions and the basic concoctions to put with the animal's feed.

We began the treatments some four weeks later. First we cleaned out the gelding's stomach and lined it with oil. Then we gave him iron and vitamin B-12 and good feed. But the vital part of the treatment was still to come: the injection into the neck of anabolic steroids.

Up to that point, to the best of my knowledge, no vet in Great Britain had ever tried these on a horse. The use of anabolic steroids was then restricted to use on humans suffering from rheumatoid arthritis—or so I was told. But that's what Georgie was using on his horses.

We started Three Gates on 2cc's every four days, for three weeks. Then we increased the dosage gradually. The effect was miraculous. The gelding perked up during the second week of treatment, got stronger and stronger, put on weight, filled out—in short, he was completely transformed.

Paddy was flabbergasted. I wasn't overly surprised, having seen it work time and again in Kuala Lumpur.

And then came the bombshell. Lady Bouverie sold Three Gates. Paddy and I had no way of knowing, but she had been contemplating the sale for some time. The gelding went to Neville Dent, a schoolmaster who'd decided to start a yard at Brockenhurst. Dent took the reborn gelding, raced him, and won.

At The Cuckoo a couple of nights later, Paddy enthused, "Kenny, do you realise what we've done? We've turned a useless gelding into a winner!"

"I know," I said, "and it's got me to thinking, Paddy. What if I used that stuff on Fantasia?"

"How do you mean?"

"Well, I'm just wondering. If those steroids and all

those vitamins build up a horse the way we've seen them do, then maybe they'll give Fantasia just that extra bit of stamina she needs to go five furlongs instead of four or four and a half."

Paddy pursed his lips. "Could be, y'know. And then you'll race her?"

"That's right. At Hawthorn."

A twinkle stole into Paddy's eyes. "Going to shrink her down to size, are you, Kenny?"

I laughed. Fantasia was 15 hands and a bit. A pony was officially 15 hands maximum, but trainers and owners got up to all sorts of tricks to get horses into pony races at Hawthorn Hill, including digging four holes in the ground, standing a horse in the holes and camouflaging the deed with straw, dung or whatever. All "ponies" were measured in their boxes well before the race by an official from Hawthorn, and not all of them had the reputation for micrometer accuracy.

This running of "ringers" at Hawthorn was a standing joke, and I intended taking advantage of it, the same as at least half a dozen other trainers. Not for the prize money, which was a derisory five hundred pounds, but for the betting, which was fast and furious with the on-track bookmakers. I saw the makings of a mini-coup, long before the coup became my way of life in racing.

After arranging for a trainer's licence, for pony racing only, I began the course of treatment on Fantasia. Nobody but Paddy Baldwin knew what I was up to, for obvious reasons. I cleaned her out, then fed her the best bran and linseed mashes. I gave her vitamin B-12 and iron for a couple of weeks and then started the steroid injections in her neck. Again, 2cc's to begun with, every four days for three weeks, then a gradual increase in dosage.

Fantasia blossomed. She was a beautiful sight to behold. Now I wanted to gallop her, but to take her up to Vernon

Cross's place would be to give away the whole show. So I made arrangements with a local farmer named Viney for the use of his land to gallop the filly. I rode her myself, although I didn't intend to for the big race. I thought I might get Morny Goodwin or Charlie Patton to ride for me.

Four days before the race in which I'd entered Fantasia I gave her a last injection of 10cc's of the steroid. She would need no more. I knew from her gallops that she was strong and ready, that she would beat anything they put in against her at Hawthorn.

My last little problem was getting her by the official who would come to measure her a day or so before the race. She was looking so fine and fit I was beginning to have my doubts about that. But all along, Paddy kept telling me not to worry about a thing. He'd fix it for me if there was any trouble.

There was trouble, all right. On the Sunday, two days before the race, the track official appeared, tape measure in hand. I brought him over to Fantasia's box. He took a look inside and spluttered in indignation.

"Bejeesus," he said, "that's not a pony. Fifteen hands six if she's an inch. I'll not pass her, Mr. Payne. I'll not even measure the beast."

I tried to remonstrate. In vain. He didn't want to know. As we stood outside the box, arguing, to the rescue came Paddy. "What's this all about now?" he said, an Irish accent appearing from nowhere.

The official explained. I protested. Paddy said, "Well, now, lads, why don't we go back into the house and argue this out over a small glass of something?"

God only knows how many small glasses of something, later we staggered back to Fantasia's box, arms around one another in brotherly love.

Paddy said to the official, "Would you like to go in there and measure the girl now?"

The official lurched, hiccupped, shook his head. "I don't know what I could have been thinking of before," he said. "Sure and the little lady can't be more than fourteen-nine. I can see that with me own eyes. I don't need to measure her at all, do I?"

We heartily agreed to that, repairing to the house for a few more things in small glasses.

So Fantasia was in. Mentally, Paddy and I were rubbing our hands in delight over the drubbing we would give the Hawthorn Hill bookies. Then there came one last hitch: my jockey. Morny Goodwin was unavailable. Charlie Patton told me he was obliged to ride a Tommy Lipton horse in the same race, which was ironic considering that Tommy had bred Fantasia.

I did have an ace left up my sleeve for just such a contingency: Josephine Clark. Jo was just about the best pony jockey at Hawthorn, and for my money could have held her own in thoroughbred flat racing had she been given the chance then. I rang her up and asked her if she'd do it. Though she usually rode for Len Dillaway, who was resident trainer for Tommy Lipton, she was free, and she agreed to ride Fantasia, sight unseen, as a favour to me. Further irony: I had a Tommy Lipton jockey on a Tommy Lipton-bred horse in a race I'm sure Tommy himself fully expected to win.

Fantasia was entered in the first race, so Paddy and I went right to work spreading our money around. I took what I could get. Fantasia was an unknown quantity but she looked so gorgeous when Jo brought her out that the odds plummeted from 10–1 to 3–1 and then to 6–1. I was feeling good until suddenly, at the parade to the post, Fantasia got fractious. She was so eager to run she was prinking about like a cat on hot coals. Jo tightened rein and Fantasia reared, took off, hurdled a fence, jumped a parked car and sent Jo flying through the air. She landed unhurt, but shaken.

We rushed to her, me, Paddy and Graham Clark, her husband. Fantasia stood nearby, pawing the ground, snorting. Jo was just picking herself and dusting herself off when we reached her. She was cursing a blue streak. "Crazy filly," she was muttering. "What the devil have you been eating?.'

I was tempted to tell her, but sighed instead, "I guess that ends our racing for today." Ruefully I began to tote up my losses; the bookmakers wouldn't return money on a horse that bolted and couldn't race.

But Jo protested. "What do you mean, ends our racing?" she said. "That filly won't beat me, Duke. I'm going to ride her, whether she likes it or not."

Graham tried to stop her. Even I began to have second thoughts. Lost money was better than a seriously injured jockey. "You don't have to get back on," I said to Jo. "Nobody will blame you for backing off, least of all me. Call it a day, Jo."

But Jo had courage, and she had determination. She was going to ride Fantasia in the race.

"If you really want to, Joe, then good luck," I said to her. "But try to waltz up to the start so you get there just as they're ready to go. Fantasia won't stand still and wait for the others. She'll take off with you again."

I held my breath then as the ponies, seven of them, walked up to the starting line. "Come on, come on," I breathed as a couple lagged behind. I could see Jo holding Fantasia back, but careful not to check her too sharply for fear she'd rear again. Three of them came up the the line, then four, then five, then Jo moved in with Fantasia, the last pony moved in beside her, and they were off! A clean start!

Fantasia took off like a shot from a cannon, as I knew she would. I'd told Jo just to let the filly go; there'd be no holding her and no need to. She'd either run away with the pack or stop short again at around four and a half furlongs.

Now I'd see with my own eyes what steroid treatments could do for a horse. At the three furlong marker Fantasia had some five lengths of daylight between her and the second horse. She was still out there and flying with four furlongs behind her. I tensed, watching, waiting for that telltale flagging, the lifting of her head as she tired.

But not this time. Not today. She streaked away, breezed home, was still going at top speed past the finish line and went another furlong before Jo could calm her, slow her, and turn her to come back down the track.

I wanted to jump up and down with excitement, but stood there, agitated, restraining myself. Paddy Baldwin came over and pounded me on the back. "It was beautiful, Kenny!" he cried. "Beautiful! What a sight to see."

A prettier sight yet was the pile of banknotes I collected after the race from a bevy of sombre bookmakers. I'd won something in the neighbourhood of five thousand pounds, which was a nice neighbourhood indeed.

And I had the feeling that it was all just beginning . . .

CHAPTER SEVEN

THERE I was, five grand burning a hole in my pocket, a successful experiment with steroids under my belt, and the wheels in my brain turning feverishly. I had long had my eye on a piece of land near Hamptworth in the New Forest, on the "Landford Level". Now I rushed out and bought it, thirty beautiful acres, with forest rights for running a string of horses, at five shillings per year per head. I was going to build a big house, and pig-pens and chicken-runs and boxes for a dozen horses. I'd breed, train, break yearlings, maybe ride a few hurdlers—who knew what I might or might not turn my hand to!

I built the house and the pig-pens and the chicken-runs and the boxes, but well before it was finished I was back to square one. Mrs. Southwell had taken back Fantasia and sold her; I ran out of money and was so deep into the bank they wouldn't advance me a penny to buy horses; Ann and I were getting on like a pair of frozen chips, and I got post-steroid depression. I began to feel I was playing with fire. So all in all, by the time I actually moved into the new place at Landford, which I dubbed Cherry Tree Farm, I hadn't a horse to my name. And did I have one, I wouldn't have touched it with steroids. It wasn't until much later that by strange coincidence the subject came up again, and my interest renewed.

My passion for horseflesh remained, however. I was up at Hawthorn regularly, betting the ponies, talking ponies and horses, wallowing gratefully in the sights and sounds and smells of a race meeting, albeit only ponies. At the same time, some of the landed people for whom I cleaned windows did begin to give me work breaking yearlings and galloping mounts. I felt all this was just a temporary setback, that as soon as I got some cash together I'd buy a small string and start myself up as a trainer. At that time, if I recall correctly, the Jockey Club insisted you had at least six horses in your string before you could get a thoroughbred trainer's licence.

Ann, poor Ann, hated it all, hated our whole way of life. I was forever trampling over the carpet in muddy boots, or sitting down to an immaculate dinner, still smelling of hog or horse. We couldn't reconcile our differences; there wasn't one point on which we could agree a compromise, or find an accommodation.

I went my own way. I found solace with other women. There's no arguing the morality or immorality of that; I did it, I admit it. It's history.

One afternoon at home I got a phone call from a very irate young lady named Lynda Jeffries, who said she was manageress for a chain of cleaning stores we serviced with window washing. She accused my workers of stealing pencils from her shops. Nothing else, just pencils. I apologised, and said I'd come around and talk to her about it, since the chain was a lucrative account. Two days later I appeared at her office in Chandlers Ford with ten dozen assorted pencils. I introduced myself and gave her the pencils. "Here," I said to her, "let my boys steal these. And I'll buy you another ten dozen when they get through this lot."

I guess she saw how ridiculous she'd been over a few pencils, because she laughed and said okay, forget it, but she'd probably had a bad day when she called and picked on me to let off steam. Then she said, "I know you, Ken Payne. You buy hay and straw from my brother Graham."

"Jeffries! That's right, Graham Jeffries!" I said. "I didn't connect the name. So you're Graham's sister!" I took another look at her, a good look, and I liked what I saw. She was about twenty, and now that I knew who she was, I knew she'd married young and had already been divorced. She was a vivacious-looking girl, very pretty, with a sensational figure.

I invited her out for a meal, and as the weeks went by one thing led to another—I was going to say, inevitably led to another, but of course there was nothing inevitable about it. It was purposeful on my part. Opportunity also presented itself at the time, because Ann was in London for several weeks on a course. She'd taken a job with Customs and Excise.

By the time Ann returned from London, I not only had a girl friend in my life, I had a horse, a stallion named Harry Flapman. He came to me from the wife of a publican friend who decided she wanted to own a race-horse. She bought Harry Flapman from Vernon Cross at Newbury one day, and sent him to me to train. I didn't have a full licence then, but I was a permit holder, which was good enough. All I had to do technically, was buy the horse from the woman; the rules allowed you to train your own horse or the horse of a close relative.

Harry Flapman never did amount to much, but it was fun having him around. I tried switching him from flats to hurdles, but couldn't make any money with him. I got as far as discussing with Paddy Baldwin the possibility of using steroids on Harry Flapman, but no further than that. He was a healthy horse, just a slow one. Steroids could give a horse strength and stamina, but wouldn't cut a fraction of a second off his real time. Eventually I got Harry Flapman to pay for his feed and board by using him to cover New Forest ponies. He was much more enthusiastic about that than he was about hurdling.

Ann took a dim view of my racing Harry Flapman. This

was not only a manifestation of her dislike for the animal farm I ran, but of her jealousy of the people with whom I associated. She didn't like racing people, and she suspected I was having affairs with some of the women in that circle. She inevitably guessed wrong and picked out an innocent girl to confront me with; it wasn't until she decided to do more than just guess that she found me out.

I believe Ann was even jealous of her young sister, Heather. The little girl I'd first met years before was almost grown up now, and the complete opposite of Ann. She was athletic, full of life, extrovert, a lover of the outdoors. She was often at our place, helping me with the pigs and the chickens, riding the horses I occasionally had in one of the boxes. Of course we gradually developed a warm relationship, built on a mutual love of our association with the animals. Ann distrusted this relationship, although Heather was still barely nubile, and to me more of a kid sister than she was to Ann herself. I wouldn't have dreamed of touching her even if she had been of age.

I regretted always that Heather was present when the crunch came with Ann; in a way, I believe the fact that she was there aggravated the situation, knowing how Ann felt about her and about our friendship. It happened on a Sunday, when Heather was at the farm to help me with the pigs, some of which were ready to drop litters.

The polite truce between me and Ann had now deteriorated to the point of open hostility. For some months I had been suffering from sporadic bouts of malaria, brought on, no doubt, by overwork and stress. Ann was unsympathetic: this was just another manifestation of my unsavoury way of living. Once, during a frightening attack that left me helpless for two days, she refused to stay home from work and care for me. Indeed, she went to stay with her mother until I recovered.

Am I displaying petulance now? I don't mean to, but this sort of thing was typical of the distasteful, spiteful warfare in which Ann and I were engaged. It was building up relentlessly, needing only a spark to set off the final explosion.

We were preparing to sit down to Sunday dinner, when Heather came rushing in to tell me a sow was having trouble delivering. The shoat was blocked in the passage.

"I'll have to go see to that," I told Ann.

"But I've just put the dinner on the table . . ."

"I can't leave the sow like that," I explained. "It'll kill her and the little piglets. Keep the dinner warm for half an hour or so. Or have yours if you want, and hold mine in the oven. I've got to see to it, Ann."

I went out to the pig-pen with Heather, and together we struggled with the squealing sow. I suppose it took me half an hour or so of messy work, but I got the job done. When we returned to the house and washed, Ann was just finishing her dinner. Mine was on the table where I'd left it, ice cold. Ann, sullen-faced, refused to look at me.

I felt all the months of suppressed anger bubble up in me and boil over. I picked up the plate of beef and vegetables and slammed it to the floor. "That's it!" I shouted. "That's bloody well it! That's what I think of your rotten dinner and this house and you and everything else that goes with you! I want you out, you understand? Out! You can take anything you want, anything you think is yours in this house you can bloody well have, but I want you out of here. We're finished!"

There was no scene. Ann was too icily polite a person to create one, or to shout back. She simply went, without a word. Heather, poor innocent Heather, went with her.

During the next few days, while I went about my business, Ann came back and forth with her car and a removal van. Bit by bit the furnishings in the house disappeared. I didn't give a damn. I wanted it all to be over and done with, and to live in peace with myself, to do my thing, work as I pleased and with whom I pleased. Within a week, Ann had completed the removal job. And complete it was; I say this with a laugh now, although I wasn't amused at the time. She left me with not so much as a mattress to sleep on. I gathered straw from Harry Flapman's box, took away one of his blankets, and slept on the floor of the bedroom. For days no one would come near me; I was rank with the odour of horse.

I felt no remorse over the separation. A sadness, yes, that it happened; regret, too, that it hadn't worked out. And when I cooled off I felt a wave of sympathy for Ann. I was a man and I could fend for myself. But I was concerned about Ann's future, and her health. I hoped fervently that this trauma would not bring about a recurrence of her illnesses.

A few months later there was a knock on the door one afternoon, and I came face to face with that stock character of broken-marriage dramas, the private investigator. I was in no mood to see him, but he told me, "Mr. Payne, it would be best for you and your wife if we had a chat. Just give me five minutes." He was so polite, I couldn't refuse him.

"Mr. Payne," he said, "in recent weeks I have gathered evidence that you are having an adulterous affair."

I was curious. "What kind of evidence?"

He consulted a notebook. "Shall I read out dates?"

I laughed. "Never mind."

He smiled. "I also have photos."

"Photos? Now wait a minute!"

He held up his hand. "Nothing obscene. Nobody was peeking in your bedroom window. But you do have this floor-to-ceiling picture window in your lounge. We obtained photos of you and other persons on the settee, not completely dressed . . . damaging enough in their implications."

That was a dity blow below the belt. Amongst those

photos there might be some of me and Heather, innocently watching television in robes or pyjamas, for sometimes she'd come over and cook a meal for me, then stay the night. I couldn't believe Ann would implicate Heather, but of course I quickly realised that she probably hand't bothered to look at the pictures and assumed they were all of me and other women.

I said to the investigator, "Look, if Ann wants a divorce, fine, I'll give her one. Why all this nasty business?"

He shrugged. "Adultery is the quickest and easiest way to get a divorce decree." This was before mere break-up of a marriage and separation was reason enough for a divorce in Great Britain.

I nodded. "Okay. I won't stand in the way. Let's get the solicitors on the job and get it done." But I did make one stipulation: the investigator had to show me the photos, and any we agreed were irrelevant were destroyed.

As part of the divorce settlement, I sold up at Cherry Tree Farm, gave Ann her share, and bought an old thatched cottage and three acres at West Wellow, near Romsey, called Blundell's Cottage. I rented an additional three acres nearby from Lynda's grandmother, for horses, and moved in, pigs, chickens, Harry Flapman—and, soon afterward, Lynda herself.

Gradually, my life returned to some semblance of normality. Lynda certainly seemed to like racing and having animals around and didn't mind my tearing around the countryside bent either on washing windows or betting on horses. I soon got another horse in my string. My father decided to buy a two-year-old filly named Lark Spring from Ralph Emery, more for breeding purposes than for racing, although race her we did, without much success.

I decided it was about time to make a serious move in the direction of a full trainer's license. With the help of such friends as Lady Bouverie and Lord Lifford, who gave me references, I applied to the Jockey Club for the license. Then, knowing the rules, I went out and bought half a dozen two-year-olds at the Doncaster sales. I remember that I bought the first six that came along, because I was in a big hurry. That very afternoon I had a big window-cleaning job to do at the home of Lord Louis Mountbatten, and I knew he insisted on my supervising the job myself.

And so the months drifted by, undramatically. Horses came and went through my little yard. I was getting nowhere fast as a trainer, holding my own, winning a race now and again, making a few quid, losing a few more, indulging my fancy with money made from the window-cleaning business. But I had no illusions about where I was going as a trainer. I knew I'd never have a yard like Atty Persse's or become another Noel Murless. My destiny was to be a "gambling trainer," one who expertly trained and ran his cheap string to win races at long odds, and make his money from the bookmakers, not from the meagre prizes offered by the tracks. But until Ralph Emery came along in 1967 with Neronton, I couldn't get it together. I didn't have the horses to put over a coup of any dimension whatsoever. I had Harry Flapman, I had Portulac, Lark Spring and Skipping in my boxes, I had no money in the bank, I had overdrafts killing me with interest. Finally I sold the window-cleaning business. It gave me a bit of cash after I'd paid some pressing bills, and it pleased the Jockey Club. They'd been after me for some time about the business, hinting politely that if I was to be taken seriously as a trainer of race-horses, then perhaps I shouldn't be gallivanting about with a ladder and bucket, cleaning windows.

The fact that it was big business made little difference. It wasn't a "class" business, I worked at it personally, big as it was, and anyway, to most of the stewards, I was a long-haired interloper in the sport of kings. So I sold the business, but in certain racing circles I was "Window" Payne forever after, even when I became the leading money-winning trainer in the North.

Some two years after my divorce from Ann, Heather phoned me one day to tell me Ann was in hospital, dying. I raced along as fast as I could, but she was dead by the time I got there. I never did find out exactly what killed her, though I inferred that her years of ill-health had taken their toll. Perhaps something had occurred to bring about a relapse. I never learned what it was, because the family refused to talk to me—all except Heather. I went around to the house before the funeral and asked if I could help with the arrangements. Ann had never remarried and her father had died the year before. I felt help was needed. But her mother slammed the door in my face. Literally.

Somehow, all these years later, I can't recall Ann's death without a twinge of guilt. At the odd moment, if I think about it or she's mentioned or, as now, I write of it, I can't escape the feeling that I share some blame for her early passing; perhaps I could have done more, could have helped her, could have been more unselfish in our relationship. But dwelling on the past bears little fruit. And horses were beginning to fill my mind totally and leave room for nothing else.

After the Neronton affair early in 1968, my "cover" was blown. Suddenly, from out of nowhere, an unknown southern trainer named Payne with a jokebook yard, developed a reputation among the bookmaerks' as a "hot number". Word gets around to these gentlemen of the turf long before owners, trainers or the Jockey Club stewards know you're even alive. All the big betting chains have informants everywhere, to keep track of heavy betting and heavy bettors. Inside information on a horse destined to win a race can kill the bookies unless they can get wind of what's up and take steps to "lay off" the bets and drop the odds.

In the ensuing months, I pulled off betting coups on new horses that came into my string: Greek Melody, Miss Camay, Cold Henry . . . then another coup with Neronton. I even managed a couple of pay-offs with Portulac and skipping. But you wouldn't catch me in a betting shop doing my own work, unless it was to put a tenner each way on a few horses I didn't fancy, just to confuse the bookies. A description of Lynda, who gambled for me, was even circulated to the shops in the entire southern area of England, from the coast to London.

I employed a few people to drive around placing bets for me when I had a coup planned. It wasn't easy. Any large bet was bound to be reported, so I had to spread five- and ten-pound bets all over the place to make a decent "kill". My system then for preparing a coup was simple enough, patterned after the Neronton killing. It was to take a horse that didn't look like much, get it into the best form possible, run it out of its class or distance to accumulate a few zeroes before its name in the form books, then find the pace it could win and make my bets.

Foolproof? Not on your life. I lost bets for all sorts of reasons, but I won more often than I lost and I was annoying the hell out of the bookmakers. They never remember the money you lose to them, only what they pay out. They became suspicious of any Ken Payne horse, but since my mounts lost more often than they won and the punters never knew when I was planning a coup, the bookies couldn't very well underlay the odds on my runners all the time, or they'd get no action. It became a battle of wits.

But I was far from satisfied with the way things were going for me. All my horses at the time were hurdlers. Hurdlers are terribly unpredictable creatures, leaping over obstacles that could not be manipulated in my favour. Hence I lost bets I should have won. Then, too, the rigours of jumping caused frequent breakdowns among the horses. I was fast becoming restless, irritable, frustrated, hankering after the glossier world of flat racing with its greater glamour and potential profit.

That is precisely when the mysterious Mr. George Pantin entered my life, and gave me the last big push forward and upward in my quest for the big money and the bright lights.

CHAPTER EIGHT

CAST your bread upon the waters, it advises somewhere in the Bible, and you'll get your just rewards. It rarely works, in my experience. More likely a good deed will get you a kick up the backside for your efforts. But at least once in my lifetime the extending of a helping hand did pay off for me, and pay off in a big way. It began at Newbury one wintry day.

Despite its elegant backdrop of woodland and rolling Berkshire countryside, Newbury always seemed to me one of the more raffish of English racecourses. Perhaps it's because of the race trains stopping almost at the paddock rails, with their lingering whiff of cigar-smoking rogues and card-sharps, and fathers exhorting young daughters not to get into compartments alone with strangers. Romantic days, those.

The track is immaculate and the course well run, but somehow there always seem to be more men than usual selling second-hand race cards and third-hand tips, or pushing slips of paper into your unwilling hands with a muted request for a quid. And Newbury also has its share of petty, self-important officials who make sure you forget you are there to enjoy yourself.

I was having a ginger ale in one of the bars after a winter day's racing when I saw one of these officious gentlemen none too gently manhandling an inoffensive drunk off the premises, threatening to turn him over to the police. I could see that the poor chap was bewildered and harmless, so I said to the official, "Look, I'll take care of him. Leave him to me."

I introduced myself to the man, a neat, dapper dresser, a little older than I and not much bigger. He told me his name was George Pantin. He said he lived in Maidenhead, and if I'd just steer him to the Lotus he had in the car park, he'd be grateful. I walked him there, but then realised he was in no condition to take charge of a pram, much less of a Lotus. So I arranged with a friend for him to take my car, and I told George I'd drive him home, then go on to mine.

"When you get around to it," I said to him, "you can come over to my place and pick up the Lotus. I'll take care of it for you, not to worry."

George was too far gone to protest. I loaded him into the car, took the keys from him and headed down the A4 to Maidenhead and the block of flats George had named. I pulled up in front of the block, and as I began to struggle with my limp passenger, now asleep in the cramped front seat, a woman emerged from the flats and gave me a hand. She said her nane was Thelma Wade. Obviously this was a not unfamiliar task for her.

Later, as I drove away through the drizzle, I wondered about the two people I'd just met. Little did I know how much influence they were to have, in their separate ways, on my racing life.

George apparently was in no hurry to pick up his Lotus. A week went by and still he hadn't turned up. I forgot about George and his car at the time, pushed the incident to the back of my mind. My primary concern was the state of my yard. My hopes of glory as a trainer were fading badly. I had lots of jumpers, but few winners and practically nothing I could depend on to give me a real coup.

My paramount frustration just then was a gelding

named Raincap. I'd bought him at the Ascot sales for five hundred pounds for Dr. Paul Bracie. The day I'd bought him, as it happens, is a day marked in permanent red in my life. I didn't make special note of it at the time, but later the significance of the day's events came home to me.

Lynda and I had been married perhaps three weeks, no more. On that morning I rose particularly early. "I'm off to Ascot now," I told her. "Remember that Dr. Bracie asking me to buy something for him? Well, maybe I can pick up a house I can use on the flat later on. See you tonight."

I'd motored twenty miles or so when I realised I'd left my cheque book home. Quickly I turned around and sped back to the New Forest. When I got to the cottage I could hear my dog barking and voices raised angrily in argument. I went in and found Lynda and her brother Graham in a fierce slanging match, shouting at each other. More than that, furniture was overturned. Dishes were broken, a lamp was knocked over.

My entrance caught them in shocked surprise. They didn't know I was there until I said, quietly, "What in the hell's going on here?"

They stared at me as though I'd been a ghost. "What are you doing here?" Lynda said to me.

"Never mind what I'm doing here," I said. "Somebody tell me what in hell's been happening in my house!"

Graham, whom I considered, and still consider, a friend, said to me, lamely, "Just family business, Ken. Nothing to get concerned about. Sorry you had to bust in on us like that."

I shook my head. "I don't get it, Graham. I mean, look at this place. What's it all about?"

But they wouldn't tell me. They remained adamant that it was just something between the two of them; it had nothing to do with me. Graham apologized for the damage and promised he'd pay for anything that was broken.

"I don't give a damn about the money," I said. "I'd just like the truth, and if it's something between you two, maybe I can help sort it out."

They remained silent. Finally I told them, "Look, I've got to get down to Ascot. I promised Dr. Bracie he'd have a horse today. I'll leave you two to get on with it, then. But for Christ's sake, remember you're brother and sister. Whatever it is, get it straightened out."

I got back into my car and took off once more for Ascot. On the way down I wondered what could have been between the pair of them to cause such violent argument. I guess I was still a bit wet behind the ears. It took me a long time to find out that the argument did indeed concern me. Graham, who was a friend more than he was Lynda's brother, had come to the house, knowing I would be gone, to accuse Lynda of giving me a dirty deal. She denied being anything but a loving, faithful wife, but Graham, as I understood it later, claimed to have names, dates and places. True or not, I never found out. But it wasn't long after our marriage that I began to develop my own suspicions about Lynda.

I guess I was better at picking winners on the racecourse than picking winners for wives.

In any case, the horse I bought that day was Raincap. The gelding had never won a race, although tried at all sorts of distances on the flat and over hurdles. He didn't look like much in the flesh, either, but I bought him for two valid reasons. First, Paddy Baldwin was also bidding on behalf of Lady Bouverie, and Paddy did not bid for junk. Second, Raincap had been pointed out to me by jockey Frank Morby.

"That's a fast horse, Duke," Frank said to me. "If you can only get him right, he'll be a winner."

That was good enough for me. But when I topped the

bidding at five hundred pounds, and led Raincap out of the ring, his trainer, Harry Hannon, laughed. "Payne, let's see you win with that one!" he challenged.

Suddenly I had misgivings. Had I made a mistake? Still, I knew deep down that if I intended to pull a fast one on the flat-racing fraternity I couldn't do it with an obvious winner. I had to try to take advantage of the fact that in the beginning I would be treated as a joke, a window-cleaner with presumptuous ambitions. Therefore I had to find horses that looked like hell, with rotten records, but with potential hidden away somewhere behind their sorry facades.

When I presented the good doctor with his prize I told him of my doubts. But I also confided: "Paddy Baldwin was after this gelding. And Frank Morby rode him and told me he had speed. He's got pretty fair breeding as well, and I think I can win with him."

Dr. Bracie, who owned a local chemical factory, was as determined as I to do in the bookies. "You go to it, Ken," he said to me. "I've lost thousands to the bookmakers and, by God, before I die I want to give them a good going over at least once."

How unfortunately prophetic he was. I had the horse to do it with, in Raincap. But by the time I was ready for the big coup with him, the doctor had passed on, barely two weeks before the race. Perhaps the doctor was somewhere where he could at least have a good laugh on the trounced bookies. I hope so.

At the time I ran into George Parltin again, Raincap was still mooning around in his box, a miserable, forlorn creature. When George finally did call to pick up his Lotus I showed him around the yard. I pointed out Raincap to him and told him the story. It was obvious to me from his manner and his comments that George knew more about horses than just the morning odds.

"Where'd you learn so much about it?" I asked him,

sizing him up. "You been a jockey at some time?"

He smiled a Mona Lisa smile. "Not exactly. But my father trained a bit in Australia."

I nodded. "I thought I detected a bit of a 'down-under' accent. Been out that way myself." I told George a bit about my Malay experiences, including my brush with horse-racing out there.

Just as well I never believed in gypsies or the occult or anything like that, believer in Fate that I am, or my blood would have run cold at the strange coincidence of the "Georgie" I knew in Kuala Lumpur, and this "George", with Australian connections, and what was next to occur with him.

That day he didn't say much, merely nodded and listened and made a few comments. He had a drink, shook my hand and departed in his Lotus.

The next day he phoned me. "Ken," he said, "I can make that horse win for you. Raincap. I can make him win."

"Yeah? How?" I laughed. "Not without a jet engine up his arse, he won't win, George."

"He'll win. If you'll do what I say. You willing to listen?"

"Of course, George. Come on out and we'll talk about it."

"I'll be there tomorrow morning. Early."

I was not overly intrigued. There are more guys on the fringes of racing with more ways to turn losers into winners than we've all had hot dinners. And that's not counting the element that will whisper to you about drugs. But I've listened to countless legal schemes, and theories on training horses, by vets, jockeys, gamblers, stewards, bookmakers and barmen. There's no secret, though, to training winners. I can give it you, free of charge, in one sentence: The right horse with the right jockey in the right race. Boom boom.

Thus, when George came around the next morning, I assumed he was bringing me either another hare-brained scheme, or some witless advice about getting a horse fit, that even the rawest of yard lads would know. Instead, he dropped an atom bomb on me.

"Kenn, you ever hear of Nandulin?"

"Nandulin? You mean steroids?"

It was his turn to be surprised. "You know about steroids?"

I laughed sardonically. "You might say that."

We compared notes on steroids and their use in connection with racing. I told George of my introduction to them in Kuala Lumpur, and he told me a bit, just a bit, about how he'd come across their use in Australia. George was absolutely, unequivocally convinced of their magical powers, combined with the same kind of regimen I knew about and had used on Fantasia: Vitamin B-12, iron and all the rest of it.

I wasn't all that convinced. I had reservations. I wasn't sure about the long-term effects on a horse's health. I knew, or at least could see, the apparent results of steroids on a horse's condition. But were there effects I couldn't see? Perhaps equally important was the question of the legality of steroids. Was it a drug within the meaning of the term specified in Jockey Club regulations?

Long before George Pantin revived the issue, I'd gone into these questions. After the affair with Three Gates and my mini-coup with Fantasia I had long talks with Paddy Baldwin about the subject. There was precious little Paddy didn't know about horses, about their anatomy, their care, their well-being. And Paddy was scrupulously honest. He would tell me only what he sincerely believed to be the facts without ever a thought of personal gain of any kind.

Paddy saw nothing wrong in the use of steroids. That is to say, more accuratrly, the use of steroids as I had used them on Three Gates and Fantasia.

At the same time I was discussing steroids with many other vets and trainers on the racing circuit. While I did not want to give away any secrets—to my knowledge nobody in Britain was using steroids on race-horses at the time—I did try to be as explicit as possible on what I had done, and might one day do again.

My story went something like this: suppose I had a horse which was in poor health, was dispirited, off its feed, uninterested in racing or anything else. And suppose I used a course of treatment on this horse that made it well again, built up its weight, its muscle tone, gave it stamina, made it eager to run—would this treatment be considered administering a drug to the horse to enable it to win a race?

The consensus view of trainers and vets was this: if I was only restoring a horse to good health, perhaps making it fitter than it had ever been before, then I was not administering an illegal drum. But time and time again I got this pertinent question: would your treatment make the horse run faster than it normally could have, for that one race only? If so, then it could be considered that you had given it a drug.

My answer to that was, and still is, unequivocal: the use of steroids on a horse *will not* make that horse run faster than it could when in good health and in peak condition.

I offered an analogy, just as valid today. If I had a window-cleaner working for me, fat, out-of-shape, short of wind, who could do ten houses a day, and I put him on a course of treatment, including steroids, which made him sound of wind and limb and able to do twenty houses a day, was I drugging him? He wouldn't be cleaning houses at an *abnormal* speed, beyond the capacity of mortal man. But he would be doing his job at the peak of his potential.

So it is with race horses. A complete course of re-building, which included steroids, never did produce new speed records. And such treatment never could. But steroids could and did turn a tired, indifferent animal into a spirited, keen, eager winner. Even animals gelded years before would get so full of themselves they'd produce stallion-sized erections. Indeed, I can recall more than one moment of desperate hilarity in the parade ring when I thought the proud reaction of a gelding would blow the gaff more surely than any test-tube back at Newmarket.

Yet for all that, the use of steroids is barred now in British racing. As I understand it, the principal argument against them is not that they are an illegal drug used to stimulate a horse to win a race (as is the use of arsenic) but that they do artificially distort the long term true form of a horse. They are also accused of causing infertility, at least temporarily. Some leading breeders claim that the use of steroids on higher-class horses affects their off-spring. If this is true, and I have yet to be convinced that it is, then I can understand a breeder's antagonism. A line has to be bred "true", even if the results don't always turn out that way.

Anabolic steroids remain controversial, whether used to improve performance on animals or humans. My own opinion is that steroids are a superb aid in restoring well-being and fitness to soured and backward horses. Steroids quickly build up weight, muscle and stamina, all of which a horse needs to perform up to its capacity on the race-course.

I do not regard steroids as a drug in the illegal or repugnant sense of the word, as it applies to racing. I do not agree with those who say it artificially distorts the horse's performance for just one race, neither do I agree with those who claim it puts unnatural strain on the horse's heart and lungs. I never saw steroids do a horse anything but good, and I used them on plenty of animals.

To be on the safe side, when I was using steroids I always gave the last injection in the series ten days or a fortnight before a race. My horses were often dope-tested but never, never found to be positive. I daresay that even using the newest tests now developed, steroids would not show up in the specimen. I know that steroids are still being used abroad, and I have yet to see a scandal break over their use.

There is no doubt in my mind that steroids used in conjunction with proper care and attention can produce sensational results. But they are no guarantee. There are more factors involved in winning a race than getting your own horse ready for it. Which helps prove my point about steroids. You couldn't take a horse that belonged in a seven-furlong selling plate, treat him with steroids, and expect him to win a mile-and-a-half for big-time stakes.

To pull off a coup still means the right horse in the right race. For the gambling trainer, the lowly Selling Race and its modest little sideshow the Auction Plate are the arenas in which to enter his champion. These are lessons I learned the hard way.

In any case, George Pantin turned me back on to steroids. He convinced me that they would make me a winning trainer in the world of flat racing, that they would enable me—and him—to pull off coups that would bring tears to the eyes of the big bookmakers. In truth, my arm needed no twisting. I was ripe, even over-ripe, for a good idea. Steroids were my shining light. Of course, the answer had been there, right in front of me, all these years. It just needed an apostle like George to point out the way. Rationalisation is a wonderful thing, isn't it?

Raincap was to be our guinea-pig. The first day he was drenched, which meant putting a pipe down his throat and sluicing out his stomach with a saline solution. His stomach was then lined with oil, and he was left alone for three days. Next he was given vitamin B-12, iron and other vitamins. My vet, Mr. Watson, a truly fine horse-doctor, was sceptical of the iron. "He'll only pass it through," he said. We kept him in the dark about most of what we were planning, and George insisted we give Raincap the iron.

"It's the whole course that does the trick," he insisted to me. "Watson doesn't know what we're doing, that's why he thinks the iron is a waste of time."

After that we began the series of steroid injections in the neck, gradually building up the dosage, as I'd done before with Three Gates and with Fantasia. And every week George would phone me and tell me to get Raincap weighed. I spent a fortune hiring horse-vans to take Raincap down to Southampton weighbridge to see how he was getting on.

Finally there was the blood count. Mr. Watson would take a sample every week and tell me the score. George was a fanatic about blood count and even wanted me to buy a machine of my own so we wouldn't need the services of a vet. I didn't go that far, but soon enough I got to understand what the blood count figures meant.

Week by week the trek to the weighbridge confirmed the evidence of my own eyes that Raincap was putting on weight. Even when we were having to gallop him every three days to keep him under control he kept on growing until he must have been half a hundredweight more horse than I had brought home from Ascot.

Most of this, as I said, was hidden from the vet. One day he said to me, "What on earth are you doing with all that B-12? You must have done all the horses in the yard twice over by now."

In fact what he thought was B-12 for all my horses had gone into Raincap alone.

After a few good gallops, and word from Mr. Watson that Raincap's blood count was right up there, we decided it was time to enter the gelding in the Spring Cup at Newbury. It was vital that we should see how he ran before putting our money on him. But it was also vital that he did not win, since no money would be on him. So we made sure he wasn't as wind fit as he might be. More important, I knew Raincap had never been in starting stalls. I took care not to educate him.

I engaged Charlie Patton to ride him, and told him, "See if you can win with him, Charlie. But don't kill the bugger doing it."

I have never told a jockey to hook up a horse. That simply is not necessary in order to ensure that your horse does not win a race. In this case I saw to it that Raincap wasn't ready, that's all. It's perfectly legal. Trainers do it all the time.

As it happened, the gelding was so fat and unschooled that he got stuck in the stalls at the start and was half a furlong behind before he figured out he was supposed to be off and running with the others. Even then, he caught up and got his nose in front at the straight among some very useful company. For a long moment there, I worried he might hang on and win. To my relief, however, he faded fast and finished well back.

But I had seen enough. I took him home and began to jump him out of the stalls next day. He was ready for the coup George and I had planned, up at Ripon. My only regret was that Dr. Bracie had died a week earlier, and would not get in on the killing. A barrow-boy named Tommy Mansfield owned Raincap now. It wasn't Tommy's style to get out to the races. He usually remained at home, tending his apples and pears. Of course I planned to tell him about the forthcoming coup, but not until just before the race. I didn't want him spreading too much money around, too soon, knocking the price down.

As for my own betting, I was already on William Hill's black-list, having relieved them of a few bob in my earlier days. But I was able to put some money around in the smaller shops, and I knew there was one bookie in the north, John Joyce, who could take five hundred or so from me and lay it off quietly without shortening the price too much.

I no longer gave money to Lynda to bet for me. Affairs between us had already come to that state.

On the day of the race, there was a crash on the motorway near Bicester, and I was late getting to the track. The horses were already parading around the ring. My nerves were tingling. I had £1,000 on Raincap at 8–1. George had staked even more. We'd got Frank Morby to ride him, Frank, who'd recommended the gelding to me in the first place. As I walked into the ring to talk to him I thought all our plans were going to collapse right then and there. Raincap was strutting around the ring sporting a mighty erection.

And now one of the stewards was coming over to speak to me. I thought quickly: It's hardly grounds for being warned off, but it could give them a clue that something unusual is happening when a gelding gets into that condition.

"Mr. Payne," the steward said with a wince, "I'd get him cut if I were you. He's rather an embarrassment."

I nodded, mentally whistling for a close call. As I well knew, of course, there was nothing on Raincap left to cut.

It was time to phone Tommy Mansfield and tell him to hurry down to the corner betting shop. Stupidly, I'd brought no change so I tried to reverse the charges. But the woman on the other end obviously thought Ripon was either in Japan or Saudia Arabia and after much shouting and confusion she refused to accept the charges. The horses were almost at the post, so in despair I sought out John Joyce and put an extra few hundred on for Tommy.

Once again—and not for the last time—I had more of my money riding on a horse than I really cared to think about. But he had a good draw and a good jockey and underneath my nervousness I had confidence. I wished George were there with me, but he'd disappeared for a few days, as was his habit.

Then they were off. Raincap leaped out of his stall with a rush, was urged to the rail by Frank and hit his stride with the leaders at the furlong marker. Frank kept him tucked in for a bit, but Raincap wanted to run. By the time they went into the famous Ripon dip Frank already had him well clear of the pack and he won going away. It was that easy.

I now had a one-horse flat-racing stable. A couple of days later this doubled when a horse box arrived from Gavin Hunter's yard with a little filly named Maori Princess. Gavin had been training the filly for George without much success, and I guess the win with Raincap convinced George that the Payne-Pantin formula should be expanded. Later many more Pantin horses were to come on to my string, including Charming Lady, Silent Valley and Atavistic—the last a distance runner with which we pulled off two big coups at Doncaster in 1970.

I actually saw very little of George, strange character that he was. Horses would arrive at my yard with cryptic messages from him about their treatment. How and again there'd be a telephone call. Then he'd appear out of the blue one morning, have a look and a chat and a drink, and disappear once more. Some two years after he entered my life, he vanished again, without a word, without a trace.

In fact, I was never quite sure who he was and whether or not George Pantin was his real name. The only time I ever saw him—or thought I saw him—in later years was when he was slipping into a Wimpole Street doctor's. I followed and asked the receptionist if that was Mr. George Pantin who'd just gone in. "No," she said, "that was Mr. Wilkinson." I left him there in his mystery. But I did hear from a couple of Australian jockeys once, that my strange friend and benefactor had been a well-known, if rather rumbustious, rider over there.

After one of his longer disappearing acts I did have the temerity to ask George where he'd been, and he said, "Oh, I had to settle something." I subsequently learned from a third party that he had flown all the way to Sydney for a private bit of vengeance on an Australian trainer. As his victim led a horse past the bar on his way to the parade ring, George appeared with a glass of beer. "Hello, old cobber," George said to the trainer. "Been away a couple of years. Have a drink to wipe away any hard feelings." And George thrust the pint of Foster's at him. It was typical of George and his faith in pharmacology that he had laced it with a terrific dose of horse purgative.

To George it had obviously been worth the return air fare to see that trainer hurtling out of the parade ring towards the lavatory, already unbuckling his belt in desperate haste.

It was several weeks after Maori Princess arrived that George appeared at the yard. Again we began with the powders and pills, plus extra pills, for good measure, to keep her from coming into season. She got the drenching, the vitamins, the iron, the blood counts, the weighing, and above all the mystic anabolic steroids. She put on weight and flourished. Her coat glistened. She was in gorgeous fettle. I was confident of another coup. Too confident.

The System, as I called our steroid treatment, would do wonders for a horse, make it feel in the pink and ready to run. But any horse still has to run against other horses, many of which are as fit and ready, some of which are intrinsically better runners. Then there are other tangibles such as your jockey, your draw for the post, the condition of the track, and the distance to be run. Not to mention that ghostly intangible, the state of your horse's mind on that particular day, no matter how ready you've got it. A filly in particular can be as mercurial as any female of any species.

I was so inflated with my success at Ripon and the appearance of Maori Princess that I forgot all these things. She was soon to give me a lesson I never again forgot, a very expensive lesson indeed.

The clerk at Salisbury, that most lovely and immaculately managed of southern racecourses, had given me permission to gallop horses on his track occasionally. Frank Morby took Maori Princess up there with a couple of local horses for a workout. After four furlongs he was practically swinging out of the saddle. It was obvious Maori Princess had improved tremendously. Frank came back and said to me, "I won't ride her."

I looked at him in astonishment. Frank was only just coming back into racing after long unemployment. I couldn't fathom his refusal of the opportunity Maori Princess obviously represented. "What do you mean, you won't ride her?" I said to him. "Why in hell not?"

"Because I know you're going to ask me to stop her. And I won't."

"Bollocks! I've never asked a jockey to hook up a horse in my life!"

"Yeah, but you don't know Mr. Pantin like I do," he said. "He's a perfectionist. He won't take your word for it she's ready. He won't risk a penny of his own money on her till he sees her run. And Mr. Pantin ain't nowhere to be found, is he?"

Frank had me there. George had disappeared again.

But I got to work and in two days of expensive telephoning I traced him to a hotel near Lake Killarney. He was there fishing with one of the two men for whom he managed the filly, Mr. Charles Raden. (The other owner was Mr. Richard I. Rack; George owned no horses, he was a manager, a middleman between owner and trainer.)

George agreed, albeit reluctantly, that Maori Princess would go for a win at Salisbury on the Saturday. He would be there with Raden and Rack.

But Saturday came and no George. No Raden and Rack, either. I was in a stew. As a novice flat-race trainer with a maiden filly I was on the boards at 20–1 with Maori Princess. Now was the time for the coup. I had a few hundred down on her, and expected to put plenty more down at the track, carefully. I had no way of knowing whether or not George had placed his bets. If Maori Princess won this one it would be ages before we'd be able to pull off another coup with her. Not only that, but another "miracle" from me like the Raincap job, and I would no longer be an unknown upstart. They'd all be on to me, and I'd never see 20–1 again on any horse I trained.

"What the hell are we going to do?" I said to Frank.

He knew the spot I was in. "Well," he said thoughtfully, "she's coming into season, you know." Which indeed she was. "Maybe I shouldn't give her too hard a ride."

I heaved a side. "I leave it up to you, Frank."

Frank's suggestion turned out to be academic. The race was a nightmare. Maori Princess contrived to be facing the wrong way at the barrier when they went off. Frank brought her around smartly and she thundered after the field. She caught up to the pack, passed them like greased lightning, and then suddenly veered across the track, practically turned around, and finally finished well down.

Toby Balding, the trainer, was next to me in the stands. "Oh my lord, Duke," he gasped. "What have you done to that filly?"

I had to admit it looked terrible, and the crowd gave Frank an awful time of it as he brought her in. I went down to the unsaddling enclosure. Red-faced, Frank said to me, "I swear to you she did it on her own. There was nothing I could do to hold her." Later we discovered that she was a filly that would veer and unsettle if you tried to move on her at all. You just had to sit still and ride her.

The stewards called me in, as I expected, and demanded an explanation. I told them what Frank told me. He confirmed it. Reluctantly, and in view of my inexperience, they accepted the excuse. But they wanted to know where she was next engaged.

"York," I said.

"Very well. We will expect her to give a good account of herself there."

So will I, I said to myself, breathing a silent prayer.

Maori Princess went back on her pills and steroid injections until George and I were confident that she would eat up the competition in a very respectable race—The Convivial—a maiden two-year-old race at York in August.

The day came, a hot, humid day, and the Knavesmire was packed with that slice of fashionable Yorkshire that seems to emerge from its rural fastness only for the Ebor meeting and the Great Yorkshire Show. I was sweating bullets, but not from the heat. There was a lot more money than I actually had, riding for me on Maori Princess, credit bets to the tune of some £6,000. I stood to win more than £30,000.

Frank got off well with the filly and gave her a hell of a terrific ride. Down the straight there was a desperate battle that had the crowd on its feet, screaming.

Lester Piggott, coming through off a low draw, beat us by a short head.

That deflating blow to the belly at York taught me a number of things. First, that it was not my lucky track—and, indeed, I never had a good run there. Second, never to gamble heavily on a horse with a bad draw. And third, always to fear Lester Piggott.

CHAPTER NINE

I HAVE known Lester Piggott since he was a boy tying up his pony at the little wooden school-hut outside our yard at Lambourn. To me he is the greatest judge of anything to do with horse-racing as well as the best jockey I have ever come across. Although it's difficult to compare him with American jockeys because the racing's different and they win so much money over there (would that they did here!) Lester must nevertheless rate as one of the world's all-time great riders.

His single-minded dedication to riding and winning I put down to breeding, with jockeys and trainers thick in both his mother's and father's families. His introverted nature I ascribe to his deafness, or just to the effects of a spartan regime—we used to joke that he breakfasted on a cough and a copy of *Sporting Life*—that has kept him at least thirty pounds below his natural weight. He is tall for a flat-racing jockey (5 feet 7½ inches) which accounts for his inimitable style.

He said to me once, "People keep asking me why I ride with my bottom in the air. Well, I've got to put the bloody thing somewhere!"

Lester has a way of dropping veritable gems of information as mere asides; he is too modest, too shy, to make an approach to you directly and say, "Here's a little something you may find valuable to know . . ." But some years back a mere mention of Tommy Lappin when I was moving my yard north gave me my best jockey; a terse, "Klairon's a good sire . . . throws genuine horses, especially the black ones," led me to take on one of the best horses I ever had, Klairon's son Kithairon; even an opinion on the next champion jockey in the paddock at York one day—"That little feller over there"—led me to back Pat Eddery and win £2,000 when everyone thought it would be Willie Carson.

I've had my share of laughs out of Lester. Like the time Snowy Wainwright stormed at him, "You'll never ride for me again," after Lester had failed to give a thrashing to a beaten Music Boy. And Lester replied, with a wink to me, "I'd better pack it in then, hadn't I?"

Lester's skills have saved fortunes and set up people for life. I remember once at Newmarket I was with my good friend and mentor Jack Doyle when he was scraping together the huge stake needed to buy the very fast Green God. This was the colt destined to be the foundation of the then unknown John Magna's great stud in Ireland. Eventually Jack got the money together, and then we learned to our dismay that owner David Robinson stipulated that Green God ran in one more race—the Vernon's Spring at Haydock—with Mr. Robinson to take the prize money.

We knew from Lester, who'd ridden the horse in France, that he was getting tired and was on the verge of going over the top for the season. Still, there was nothing to be done about it, except withdraw from the purchase, which Jack was loathe to do. Buying the horse and letting him run in that condition was a calculated risk; if he were beaten, especially if he were badly beaten, it would greatly reduce his value against the price Jack had agreed to pay.

Lester was engaged to ride him and he said to us before the race, "You won't see me till the very end, so don't go getting heart failure."

Jack is normally an unflappable man, cool and confident. I have seen him wheel and deal with some great horseflesh, notably Right Track, Bruni, Mill House and Sandford Lad, to name only a few. But he was nervous that day at Haydock, and indeed there was neither hide nor hair of Green God and Lester to be seen as the pack rumbled into the final furlong. We were convinced it was impossibly late for Lester to make his move. But then, there he was, bum in the air, threading his way between horses to bring the colt home to win by the shortest of heads.

All he did, when he walked in, was give us the smallest ghost of a grin.

Now and again Lester used to ride gallops for me when I'd moved my yard to Lambourn, but rarely did he ride races for me. My platers were not in his league. However, one day I read in the papers that Lester was coming slumming up to Pontefract to try to sew up the jockey championship in that unlovely shadow of Ferrybridge power station and the local corporation tip. I was not surprised, therefore, when the telephone rang and he was on the line enquiring if I had any runners that might do him some good. I duly put him on a couple of winners and was happy enough to give him a tiny leg up towards the title.

By then I figured maybe it was time Lester did me a favour, without his necessarily knowing about it. I had a horse named Big Jake which I had set up for a race at Warwick. There was always something especially sweet about a coup at Warwick because the bookmakers there had a long-standing feud going with me. Indeed, it was there, one balmy spring afternoon, that an incensed member of the brotherhood had literally hurled my winnings at me, sending me scrambling round in the mud for £500. That kind of humiliation I could always bear.

But I was determined to unbutton the bookies there once again, and this time I would use Lester, albeit unwittingly, as my bait. I put John Curant, my No. 2 jockey, on my No. 1 horse, Big Jake, and I engaged Lester to ride another horse out of my stables, Mr. Bojangles. He'd never shown much, and I made double sure he wouldn't show against Big Jake by leaving him in his box for a week before the race. No way would he be fit.

The combination of Piggott on a Payne horse was too good for the bookies to miss. They smelled a miracle afoot on Mr. Bojangles, and rapidly shortened the odds on him. Meantime the odds on Big Jake drifted out. I could hardly contain my laughter. To add to the camouflage I strolled around the ring betting a few hundred on camouflage I strolled around the ring betting a few hundred on Mr. Bojangles, berating the bookies for their gutlessness on creating such short odds on a horse that had shown nothing. The sneers I got from the bookies who thought they had plugged up my coup utterly delighted me.

While all this diversion was being created, friends and allies were pouring money on to Big Jake all over the country, in unspectacular single bets and little corner betting shops.

I knew that at some point Lester would twig that it was all a set-up; probably as he tried to get a puffing Mr. Bojangles to give him an extra ounce of effort. But I was unprepared for him to beckon me over when he had only walked the animal once around the parade ring. I had already given him stern orders to win. I went up to him, my heart in my mouth, hoping he wouldn't be cross with me. I looked up at him, questioningly. In reply he said not a word, just pushed his cap back and gave me a wide grin.

What I hadn't allowed for was Lester's phenomenal judgement of any horse, from selling plater to Derby winner. As soon as he swung into the saddle. and nudged the horse he knew Mr. Bojangles wasn't fit and hadn't a snowball's chance in hell of winning that race.

It was a ferocious race, as it transpired, and I began to worry as soon as the horses came around the home turn a couple of furlongs from the post. Curant was already showing Big Jake the stick. But despite a mighty effort down the straight my horse was beaten by a head. There was a time when this would have been an unmitigated disaster for me, but amongst other things I'd learned down the years was that when the odds were long enough it paid to hedge a bet by putting money each way (betting place as well as win).

In any case, all regrets over fortunes lost and the foiling of what I must confess I considered one of my more elegant contrivances were put aside by the sight of Lester and Mr. Bojangles sailing insouciantly up the middle of the track a good hundred yards in arrears. His feet had hardly touched the ground in the unsaddling enclosure before we were both ushered into the Stewards' Room. They demanded an explanation for such a performance from the great Piggott.

Lester shrugged; then, in that Mickey Spillane voice of his which he saves for his best pronouncements, he said to them, "De guy's a nut." He turned to me next and said, "Next time you want me to ride a racehorse, get it fit."

There wasn't much the Stewards could say, except to give Lester a right rollicking for appearing in their august presence without a shirt on and with just a towel around his neck. They dismissed him then. I was much relieved, because the last thing I wanted was for Lester to suffer for an attempted coup about which he knew nothing—at least until he'd sat on the horse.

As for me, I explained to the Stewards that Mr. Bojangles was not a boy's ride and I didn't think Curant could handle him. True enough, I knew the horse needed a race but the owner wanted him to run at Warwick and, well, horses always need races, don't they? That last part, of course, was left unsaid but understood. Owners and trainers are constantly giving horses exercise in races to get them fit, otherwise the tracks could never fill out a card. It's part of racing; it's good for the horse, the trainer, the track—for everybody but the punter who thinks the horse is out there to win. But that's another story.

Perhaps the Stewards on that day didn't quite accept my explanation of events. But they dismissed me without comment.

As I emerged, the jockeys' valet was waiting with a message to say that Mr. Piggott wanted to see me after the racing was finished. I met him later and he said to me, "That horse of yours. A couple of gallops and he'll be ready to win, you know. But you better hadn't do it too soon, or you'll be taken to Portman Square to meet the Jockey Club in a ball and chain."

That really surprised the hell out of me. I didn't reckon Mr. Bojangles at all. "Well, what do you think I should do?" I asked Lester.

"Let me think about it," he replied. Then he said goodbye and vanished.

A week or so later he phoned me. "You got him entered for that race at Kempton. Declare him. Run him."

He was talking about a £2,000 seller coming up. I knew there were some respectable horses expected to go. "I don't know, Lester," I said. "There're at least four in there he can't beat."

"They'll never run. You declare him," Lester said. And hung up.

To this day I have no idea how Lester knew—maybe he'd simply called the trainers and asked them—but when I opened the paper in the morning there were only two horses left in. Mine and Waterville, with Pat Eddery up. I could hardly believe it. Well, I'd have to be either first or second, although naturally there'd be no place betting. And the odds would be short on Mr. Bojangles, despite his poor form, with Lester riding him again.

To keep the odds at least about even, I had some of my confederates lay money on Waterville all around the place, while others put money on Mr. Bojangles. I had a connection going then in Jamaica as well, and arranged for money there to be bet for me on my horse. As the jockeys were mounting; Waterville was 5–4 on, while Mr. Bojangles was 11–10.

From the saddle Lester said to me, "Got a couple bob on him, have you?"

"Yeah. A bit," I said.

"Give yourself a birthday," Lester said. "I'm sure you could use it. He'll win it."

If Lester Piggott tells you he's going to win a two-horse race, then he's going to win it. I'd pawn my gold fillings on it. "But," I pointed out, "there's no time to get any more down, Lester. You'll be called to the start in a minute."

At that he leapt off the horse and started ranting and raving at the stable lad who was with Mr. Bojangles. "If you want me to ride a horse, get his girths done up properly and his saddle in the right place!"

While the commotion was going on I ran off and put another few hundred on my horse. Good old Lester.

The melodrama was far from over. As I'd told the stewards at Warwick, Mr. Bojangles was a man's ride. I hadn't lied about that. He was a cantankerous horse and would only put up with being schooled at all by two of our oldest hands. Everyone else was promptly deposited on the ground. That afternoon at Kempton he was in no better mood.

When the two horses jumped off Mr. Bojangles kicked, bucked and threw Lester right forward so that he lost his irons. Luckily for me my money was riding on the hands of a great craftsman. Lester rides short in any case, but he just sat there, took his time and recovered his stirrups, and by the last furlong he had his mount well in hand. He won by half a length looking back at the other horse.

A few more of my bills got paid.

Lester is unique. Not for nothing is he known to the betting shop punter as "The Guv'nor"—the best. Maybe I have a special place for him in my personal pantheon of immortals because like me he has had his brushes with the Stewards of the Jockey Club. Some punters don't like him because they say that in a cheap race on a cheap horse he won't make a supreme effort to win. That's rubbish. True, he will not beat a horse half to death when he knows it's been beaten—and he does know, make no mistake about that. All the punter with money on the horse sees, is Lester apparently easing up in the straight. But that is not the case. The fact is that the horse has had it, has run its race and can do no more. A thrashing with the whip might look good from the grandstand, but Lester does not ride for cosmetic effects.

There was a great jockey in America who used to suffer from the same sort of criticism from the unsophisticated punter. His name was Eddie Arcaro, who was to American racing in the late 1940's and early 1950's what Lester is to British racing in this generation. It was often said of Arcaro, as it was and still is said of Lester: in a big race you bet the jockey, not the horse. The exaggeration is very slight indeed.

Good jockeys there are aplenty. But many of them are good only on good horses. What separates them from Lester is his feel for anything from a Derby winner to a milk-float hack. One minute he can be riding Nijinsky, the next he can be on a really bad horse in a seller and he can still say to the trainer. "Put him in at Newcastle, and he's got a chance."

Lester once rode one of the most cussed animals I ever trained and nearly got us both lynched at Pontefract. The horse was called Perfect Nonsense, a name that described its behaviour perfectly. He was well enough bred and I bought him cheap at Ascot sales from a rather desperate, twitchy gentleman who looked immensely relieved when the auctioneer's hammer fell for what seemed to me a relatively paltry sum. Once I'd signed the cheque, the chap gave me the lowdown on his animal. It turned out that he had bred the calf, let him out for a little canter around the Romney marshes, and then couldn't catch him. For the best part of a year the animal had galloped free over the marsh, having the time of his young life. However, with the coming of winter the pinch of hunger had brought him close to home, looking for a handout. The breeder caught him, collared him, wintered him, then whipped him off to the sales ring at the earliest opportunity.

As the man took the cheque from me, shaking the ink dry, he said, "Just don't turn him out in anything bigger than a play-pen."

If romping over the marshes had been his only touch of lunacy we would not have complained. Horses can be as queer as people. But Perfect Nonsense turned out to have an extremely individualistic attitude towards racing; he seemed stubbornly to resist the idea that the name of the game is to finish in front. Yet we knew from his gallops that he was very fast, and good enough to dispose of the moderate opposition I usually contrived to arrange for his sort.

More in desperate hope than in expectation I asked Lester to ride him in a race at Pontefract. I figured that if anything at all could sort him out it would be the Piggott magic. I wouldn't bet a penny on him, of course. Nobody at the yard, or anybody else I knew anywhere, had a farthing on him, but that did not stop the enticing combination of Piggott and Payne from once again seducing the bookies and the punters. Perfect Nonsense went off at a ridiculously short price.

Lester got him well placed in the early running. Then, coming past one of the larger Pontefract slag heaps into the dog-leg signalling the home straight, Perfect Nonsense stuck his nose out in front. I reflected ruefully that I had not wanted Lester to be quite that good at handling the horse. But at least the crowd seemed to be pleased, loudly urging Lester on. Suddenly, when he had half a length in hand, Perfect Nonsense turned his head and practically stopped running. The pack rushed past him, and he was left nowhere.

As a tight-lipped Lester rode him in to unsaddle, he was surrounded by a jeering crowd, with just that touch of nastiness that affects a Yorkshireman when he thinks he's being unfairly deprived of a ha'penny. The jostling and the catcalls continued as we marched to keep our appointment with the Stewards.

Lester was belligerent, rather than defensive. I didn't have to say a word, after he told them, "If that horse tried as hard to win as his jockey and trainer, he would win the Derby."

The horse was just a petulant and erratic creature with a will of its own. And where winning was concerned, its will determined that it wouldn't. However, Lester had tumbled to this fundamental weakness in the colt's character. There are horses like that—they hate winning. What it really amounts to, of course, is that once out in front they lose interest in the race and no amount of urging on the jockey's part can get them going again until the other horses catch up and pass. By then the race is over. That was Perfect Nonsense. He would gallop hard enough to pass six or seven horses, but then stop and turn his head as if to say, "Hey, where'd they all go?" And they'd all go right past him.

Recognising this, Lester said to me, "Next time try holding him up till the very last minute, then let him go so that he passes the rest of them just before the winning post. But you'll have to time it dead right, otherwise you'll be stuck again with the stopping and looking around business."

Soon afterward I declared Perfect Nonsense for a race at Catterick. Unfortunately Lester was away in France, coaxing a grand prix performance out of some aristocratic animal in a big race there. I could hardly expect him to cancel in favour of another chance to ride my lunatic colt upon the playing fields of Catterick. So Frank Morby was given the job of putting Lester's advice into practice. Once again I tooled up the A1 in search of the pot of gold. This time I had spread a bit of money around on Perfect Nonsense. With the odds hanging about at 12–1, the attractions overwhelmed any doubts I had that Frank could achieve the perfect timing needed to make a winner of Perfect Nonsense.

Halfway up the motorway my car broke down. I was frantic. No matter how fast the RAC might get there, we'd never make it in time for the race. Just then a chap pulled up in a brand new Ford Capri with trade plates on.

"Where you going?" he asked us.

"Catterick," I said. I introduced myself and then Frank, telling the chap we had to get up there for the first race.

"Hop in," he said. "We'll make it."

The car had eighteen miles on the clock. "I'm just delivering this," the chap said. "A little detour won't hurt it."

I've made some fast runs up the A1 in my time, especially when I was driving my E-type. But this chap really gave us a ride. We must have been doing over a hundred all the way and as we pulled off Catterick roundabout and on to the track there was a sinister-looking, milky fluid leaking from the bonnet. Frank dashed off and weighed out with one minute to spare. I stood and looked at the steaming Capri. The driver said, calmly, "Looks as though it'll have to get a new engine."

I felt sorry for him. "Look," I said, "have you ever been racing?"

"No. Never."

"Well, have you got any spare cash on you?"

"Yeah, I always carry a bit for emergencies."

"Come on, then."

I took him by the arm into the enclosure and made sure he got the best price going. Then we went up into the stands. There isn't much to divert you from the racing at Catterick, so we had no time to stiffen our resolve for the ordeal ahead. We'd hardly got settled before they were off and running.

Catterick can be a right bastard of a track, with its tight bends and inclines, without adding the torments of a mean-minded horse. And it is a very fast track. Even so, we had plenty of time to appreciate what was happening to our investment. Perfect Nonsense had a nice economical stride so he was not unduly troubled by the natural hazards, but almost from the first the field divided into two bunches. Frank had Perfect Nonsense at the back of the first bunch, well placed. But I had one or two nerve-racking moments wondering whether my colt might consider that he had done enough by being ahead of the second bunch.

"Is he doing?" my Capri driver said to me nervously.

"Great, great," I said, wishing I meant it.

Frank kept Perfect Nonsense at the back of the bunch until, like Lester himself that day on Green God, it was beyond reasonable expectations that he could do it. Then he gave the colt one good crack with the whip, and Perfect Nonsense began to eat up ground.

It was a close-run thing, as somebody said at Waterloo.

Not only did Perfect Nonsense get up by the shortest of heads, but his hindquarters were barely past the post when, sure enough, he turned his head, stopped racing and was already pulling up to a walk as the rest of the field went thundering past him. By the time the last horse came galloping home Perfect Nonsense had called it a day and was leading Frank back toward the racecourse stables.

I got my money off the course—close to fifteen grand. The guy with the car got £1,200. Somebody got a Capri with a burnt-out engine. And Lester got a telegram of thanks from me.

All in all I think his wife summed up Lester best. She said of him, "He's as close to being a centaur as any man could be."

CHAPTER TEN

Race-horse owners are a breed unto themselves, sometimes as capricious and highly strung as the horses they own—if not more so. People come to own racehorses for all sorts of reasons, usually not connected with the making of money. There are of course the genuine lovers of horses and of sport, the breeders and the owners of Derby winners, and the Royal stables. And there are the little people, the farmers, tradesmen, business executives and such, who love the game and hope each year that they'll at least break even and be able to stay in it. The prestige and status of owning a race-horse is not to be underestimated. Not for nothing does racing boast the proud sobriquet, the Sport of Kings. There are some people, who can afford to use, and don't mind losing, thousands on their stables each year, just for the privilege of wearing that owner's badge.

A gambling trainer like myself inevitably wound up with some owners who needed a coup as badly as I did just to remain solvent. Fortunately I've had my share of well-heeled owners as well as those who somehow could never quite remember to pay the feed bill. But rich or poor, on the edge or substantial citizen, I must say that with rare exceptions the people I trained for were first-rate. Characters, yes. But first-rate people.

Every morning these days, as I leave my London flat, I walk past the expensive little cul-de-sac of Devonshire

Mews, where an early lesson in the hazards of race-horse ownership was literally knocked into my head under a rain of pots and pans. The whims and caprices of owners have lost me many a race and even more gambles: Larry Parnes, Tommy Steele's manager, dreaming of useless winners; Chummy Gaventa vetoing a coup because it was a Jewish holiday; Douglas Lowry taking offence at a jockey's taciturnity and turning him off; Tom Umpleby killing a coup with kindness. But I have to confess that the graduation course, in handling owners and hustling desperately needed winners, that began that night in Devonshire Mews, was largely my own doing.

One of my owners, Michael Knowles, was getting married, and we went to the Blue Angel Club to celebrate with Richard Hannon, the Marlborough trainer (Harry Hannon's son). I knew that the celebration might have overtones of a wake, since Michael's beloved was enamoured neither of me nor of horse-racing. But I hardly anticipated that the last rites would be so soon upon us. By the end of the evening Richard and I had acquired two girls and were faced with the usual problem of where to take them. Michael rescued us. His fiancee had bought a new flat opposite her old one, in preparation for married life. We could use that.

The place was newly decorated, there were early wedding presents littered all over the place, and although one or two essentials were missing, like beds, I did notice the thickest, whitest, long-pile carpet I'd ever seen. Clearly the workmen had not quite finished, for on the toilet door was a notice, saying: "Please do not use the flush. Decorator."

Michael said, "For heaven's sake don't make a mess," and retired to one of the rooms.

It was still dark when I heard an awful yell and the sound of crashing and banging. I rushed out into the corridor to see Richard in his underpants with a solid jet of water hammering into his face. He was desperately fighting to put the lavatory cistern back on the wall. I could see it was a losing battle. The white carpet was already sinking beneath the waves. There didn't seem to be any cut-off tap and the only solution that occurred to me was to try to sweep the flood out into the corridor of the block of flats. The commotion and the lights on in her new flat at that hour must have disturbed Jane, for she came running over to see what it was all about. I can imagine her feelings upon opening the door to find a rather sheepish finance, two men in their underpants and two underdressed and overendowed girls trying to sweep a tide of water out of her bridal chamber.

I was not surprised when she began to scream, curse and cry, in mixed order and for some moments all at once. And then, in case her voice had not carried all the way to the nearest police station in Marylebone, she leapt to the phone to summon every possible emergency service in the West End.

The police arrived first and stood around in muted hilarity. The fire brigade turned up, decided they were the wrong brigade and went away, after calling for the right brigade. Meantime Richard and I continued to sweep the water down the only visible drain—the lift shaft. Finally a white-helmeted Fire Chief arrived on the scene of this Mack Sennett classic, and pressed the button to summon the lift. I looked out the window just in time to see him stagger back in a great blue flash as the lift motor blew up in the pool of water at the bottom.

I got the feeling we were not going to be of any further help, so I motioned to Richard, and the two of us fled the flat in our underpants, with Jane leaning out the window hurling curses and pots and pans at our heads. I found time to wonder whether any of the copperware was a wedding present.

The next day I received the inevitable message from

Michael: He was unable to pursue his interests as a race-horse owner, and would I like to buy the horse of his that I was training, King's Crunch?

King's Crunch was a gelding which had never had a chance to be troubled by the charms of the opposite sex, but the hapless animal was to find that the charms of the girls from the Blue Angel had launched him on as hectic a merry-go-round as ever I inflicted on a horse.

At the time, I was going through one of those all-too-frequent patches when the odd thousand or two was not readily available for buying race-horses. So it was essential that I find another owner for King's Crunch. I knew that, though immature, he was a horse with definite capabilities and possibilities, a horse with which I could land a coup one day. I didn't want to let him get away, but somebody was going to have to write Michael Knowles a quick cheque and be able to pay the feed bills. Fortunately I knew a businessman named Ted Peskin who loved whipping the bookmakers and who had the ready cash. Assured by me that King's Crunch was a horse for a coup, he agreed to buy.

I gave the gelding the full treatment—drenching, vitamins, steroids—and once again chose Catterick for a coup. I had him entered for a quiet little selling race at the start of a Thursday afternoon card. I planned a final gallop on the Sunday before and a leisurely trip up on the Wednesday. I was confident he would trot up a winner—until I got a phone call the week before the race from Peskin. He had a relative coming over from Ireland for the weekend and he wanted the horse to run at Sandown on the Saturday. I'd had him entered but hadn't intended running him then, of course.

I protested. "You know he's ready for the Catterick gamble," I said to Peskin. "He doesn't need the race, and if he does at all well he'll kill the price for us at Catterick." But Peskin was adamant. He wanted to show off his horse to his relative.

There was nothing I could do. However, I took it philosophically. I rationalised that the race would serve as the horse's final gallop and I'd tell my jockey Frank Morby not to punish him if he didn't feel like running. I also figured that by the time I'd popped open a bottle of champagne in the owners' bar with Ted and his relative and they'd each had a few glasses of the bubbly, the requirements of hospitality would be satisfied. There'd be no nonsense from Ted about asking King's Crunch to try for the impossible.

Despite all the treatment he'd had from me, King's Crunch was still a big gangly sort, and I was standing in the paddock wondering how he'd manage the sharper turns at Catterick on Thursday, when Frank Morby appeared, dressed in his street clothes. In answer to my open-mouthed surprise, he volunteered, "The owner has jocked me off, gov'nor. He's putting up Ray Reader."

Ray Reader was a journeyman jockey, but no Lester Piggott or Joe Mercer, and so the message was loud and clear. Ted Peskin wanted his horse to win and he did not trust me, quite justifiably, to send Morby out there with instructions to produce the horse's best.

When Reader came out and mounted up I tried my last stroke. "Look here," I said to him sternly. "don't you dare knock that horse about. You haven't a hope of winning, and I don't want him put off racing for life."

Watching from the stands I saw Reader jump him off all too smartly and settle him down quickly. But then he took King's Crunch so wide toward the railway I thought he was going to need a platform ticket for Esher station. That ended his chances for a win, but in the final furlong he was going like the wind. In private dismay I envisaged what Timeform's summing up would tell the world: "Fast finishing fourth in Sandown maiden." A remark like that could easily make him a favourite in a modest

Catterick seller.

Back in the unsaddling enclosure after the race, Reader jumped off and announced his verdict to Peskin: "He'll never amount to much."

Peskin frowned at me, and I told him defiantly, "That's the best horse you'll ever own." But I hardly expected to convince him.

He didn't even give me time to get home to the New Forest before he was on the phone telling Lynda that he wanted to sell the horse. Wearily I dialled his number, bargained him down to £1,200, and went to bed. My brain was numb. The prospects for the week ahead were not exhilarating. I was short of cash to pay the staff anyway. Now I'd bought a horse from a disappointed owner who wanted his cash on the barrel-head, and my prime asset, the Catterick coup, already seemed shot full of holes.

The Indians appeared to be dancing ominously around me, ready to detach me from my scalp; I could only hope that the U.S. cavalry would come charging to the rescue in the last reel.

But the King's Crunch affair began as Mack Sennett comedy and it was to continue Mack Sennett, rather than John Wayne.

The action began at three o'clock the next morning with a Peter Sellers voice talking to me over a crackling telephone line. "Delhi calling Mr. Payne. Delhi calling Mr. Payne. Do you hear me, sir? Delhi calling Mr. Payne." Then after a series of whistles, bangs and gurgles and what sounded like the immersion of the phone in the Bay of Bengal, Dr. Desai came on the line.

Dr. Desai owned a sharp little filly named Misfit that I was preparing for a coup the following month. His business was exporting railway parts to India from an eagle's eyrie of an office looking out on Nelson's column in Trafalgar Square. Come to think of it, make that a pigeon's eyrie. In any case it was a good business; obviously the Indian engines broke down often enough to support my training fees and to make a small annual contribution to the Newmarket bloodstock sales. Normally Dr. Desai was content to worry about 4–4–0 locomotives and leave me to worry about his horses. But this morning it was different. He had had a dream that his filly was going to win at Epsom the following day (I had her entered for a gallop). He was forthwith cancelling his business trip and flying home at once to see her run.

I reckoned Dr. Desai's dream was born out of an over-indulgence in mutton curry, because that filly would have needed a boost from an Air India jet to win the Epsom race. But there was no arguing with Dr. Desai's dream. He was coming home.

Epsom had always seemed to me better left to the gypsies and the hucksters: an eccentric track suited to freakish horses, buried in the straggling outback of South London and guarded zealously by traffic jams. It was no different that Monday as I sat becalmed in the doldrums of another snarl-up on the South Circular Road. Not a whiff of anything that might get the traffic moving, just noxious fumes. I resigned myself to the start of a bad week.

In the immobile vehicle next to me sat a man in the uniform of British Rail. I called out to him, "You think we'll ever get moving?"

He shrugged expressively. Who should know better about immovable objects than a man from British Rail? "Where are you going?" he asked.

"Epsom. I'm supposed to be saddling a horse in the second race."

"Well, look," he said, "I'm the guard on the next train to Epsom. Come with me. You can leave your car in the station car park and pick it up on the way back. You'll never make it in this traffic."

I was tempted to make a witty return about people in

British Rail uniform not throwing stones, but generously thought better of it. He was right about the traffic. The South Circular Road, I'm sure, was designed for pony and trap, not the automobile.

As I climbed onto the train some weary minutes later, the price of a day return to Tattenham Corner Station seemed a bargain indeed. Apparently my fellow traveller on the seat opposite had thought so, too. He was blockaded behind a wall of form books, racing papers and index cards, just the top of his trilby showing above the parapets. From behind it all came the sound of mumblings and incantations, as though a lama were at prayer.

"Looking for a winner?" I said brightly. I could be friendly, if not original.

He lowered his defences, and I perceived at once the face of a desperate man. "I've got to find one," he said. "I've got to. I've done three grand to the bookies in the past week."

My compassion was aroused. Normally I do not give tips to strangers, but doubtless I was so bemused by carbon monoxide poisoning and the plush appointments of the British Rail carriage that I forgot where I was and confided my secrets to the desperado in the trilby. I told him my horse would not win, gave him my choice for the probable winner of the seller, and parted company from him at Epsom station. As I was going into the track I heard someone being dressed down by the gateman for using the wrong entrance, in tones suggesting the Crown Jewels were under assault. It was my friend of the form books and trilby. I gave him my badge and ushered him inside.

It was a predictable afternoon. Dr. Desai's filly lost, my tip in the seller won, and the tea tasted like dishwater. Going back on the train to liberate my car I met the form-book fanatic once again. He was effusive in his praise for my clairvoyance. Not only had he recouped his losses, but he had rung up his partner in London, got some more money down off-course and they had turned a bad week into a birthday party. I gave him my card, and thought no more about it.

I had already decided that I would have to run King's Crunch again at Brighton the following day in order to have him beaten. Unless he had a nought before his name there was no hope of getting the kind of odds I needed to make the Catterick coup worth while. And a Catterick coup had become a financial necessity. Even though it meant running King's Crunch three times in a week and shuttling him from the New Forest to the South Coast and then up to North Yorkshire, I was certain I could pull it off. Up north he would be a whole class ahead of the field.

The complications of this business with King's Crunch were giving me a headache, but there was yet more clutter to come. Richard Hannon phoned me. His credit was even worse than mine at that moment, so could he borrow my horse-box to take a runner up to Wolverhampton while I hired one to go to Brighton? He would be flush enough by the time the bill came in to pay me. "Sure," I said. "Why not?" I don't suppose it occurred to me that his horse might lose at Wolverhampton and I'd get stuck with the bill for the box, but then I always was a bit soft in the head about those things where friends were concerned.

Before I set off for Brighton, there came another phone call. It was from my friend at Epsom, to thank me again and to tell me he was putting a present of £500 in the post.

"Forget the £500," I said. "If you've got another seven hundred you can own a racehorse that's running at Brighton this afternoon, and by the day after tomorrow you can get all your money back with interest. Have you got the cash?"

"Well, yeah, thanks to you, I have," he said, apparently

slightly disconcerted by my whirlwind approach.

"Right. You've got to stick that £1,200 in readies through a letterbox in Marlow-on-Thames before eleven o'clock this morning and get the form signed saying you're paying for all the horse's engagements."

When I rang from a call box near Lewes at midday I found I had acquired a new owner and would be able to pay off Peskin.

I had no fears that anything would go wrong at the Brighton race. It was seven furlongs, and King's Crunch needed a mile. And just in case there was any chance of him hanging in there with the leaders, I knew that with his ungainly stride the Brighton hill would finish him off. he finished fourth in the seller, showing nothing to encourage the newspaper writers to pay attention to him next time out. I descended from the stands, wading through the jetsam of whelk cartons and fish-and-chip wrappers that always make the place look more like the beach below the West Pier than a race-course. Suddenly I heard the last sound in the world I wanted to hear, the Tannoy summons to the weighing room which invariably means someone has claimed your horse out of the seller and it's going to cost you dearly to get him back.

To explain a selling race as briefly and as simply as possible, it's a race in which any horse running can be "claimed," that is, bought, by anybody, at the set price of twice the winning purse plus one hundred guines. Thus if a race is a £750 seller, for example, anybody can claim any horse in it for £1,500 plus 100 guineas. If the original owner or trainer wants to keep the horse, he has to bid against the claimant. Any surplus over the set price goes back to the track, so the courses love these little auctions. Often the clerk of the course will use someone to drive up the bidding. I've seen as good a clerk as John Sanderson of Catterick take bids over the phone.

I walked into the clerk of the course's office for the auction, to find myself facing, of all people, Richard Hannon's father, Harry. He had heard from Richard that I thought highly of King's Crunch and he had brought along a builder friend of his called Ken Gurlen to buy him out of the race. Mentally I cursed the entire Hannon family unto three generations. Bitterly I thought of my own horse-box carrying a Hannon horse to the races at Wolverhampton. It was Richard who'd landed me with the rig in the first place by flooding Michael Knowles' flat; now he was trying to deprive me of the animal.

Well, maybe he thought he was doing me a good turn. Be that as it may, his father bid me up stubbornly, and it cost me a thousand poinds paid to the course to get back the four legs I counted on to carry me back to solvency in two days' time. I got over the difficulty of having not even a hundred pounds to pay for him, much less a thousand, by deliberately writing the cheque wrongly. By the time it would be returned I anticipated being well in funds.

Came the Thursday, and my confidence was dented. In the paddock at Catterick, King's Crunch looked awful. He had clearly lost a lot of weight from all the travelling. Even among an undistinguished bunch of northern also-rans he hardly looked a winner. Still, I had everything going for me. I'd even engaged a good young apprentice to ride him, Willie McCaskell, in order to gain the extra seven pounds apprentice allowance. I told Willie to tuck King's Crunch in and not to let him go until the final furlong.

As they paraded to the post King's Crunch seemed to be keen and full of beans, and my spirits rose. All was not yet lost.

They got off smartly, but I could see that Willie was having trouble. King's Crunch wanted to run, and with still two furlongs to go he rushed into the lead, with Willie crouched helplessly on his back like a flea on a rabbit.

There wasn't a horse within five lengths of him when he flew past the post and he careered on for another half a circuit before Willie could persuade him that the action was over.

As he got off to weigh-in, Willie said, "Guv'nor, I couldn't hold him any longer. I was real scared that he was going to jump right over the rails. It's the first time I've sat on a flat-race horse that wanted to run a steeple-chase."

There were no questions from the stewards, and much quiet rejoicing throughout the land. I had £3,000 in credit bets spread around at 3–1, which put me back in the black for the moment, anyway; the owner had recouped his £1,200 with plenty to spare; and I had learned another lesson about the vagaries of owners.

From that time on, I always tried to keep a share of the ownership of any horse I valued, in order to minimise the extent to which I was at the mercy of an owner's whim. In theory it was a great idea, and it worked well for years. At the same time it was an awful capital expense, and it contributed to my eventual downfall.

Still, no matter what precautions I took, it was next to impossible to protect myself at all times from the eccentricity, if not downright lunacy, that seemed to afflict so many owners. In fairness, I suppose I must add that while a touch of lunacy is not necessary for race-horse ownership, it certainly does help. Especially with the price of feed these days.

Often the shrewdest of horsemen had some private obsession that occasionally obscured their judgment. Even one of the best horses I ever trained, Kithairon, was tripped up once by an absurd caprice of his owner. Kithairon had caught my eye at Newmarket sales because he was by the French stallion Klairon, which Lester Piggott had once recommended to me. But he had a reserve of £3,000 and, as Jack Doyle pointed out to me, he was inelegantly long in the pasterns. This gave him rather an ungainly appearance.

I bid for the horse, then dropped out, and the reserve wasn't met. Afterward the owner came up to me and asked if I was still interested. The owner was a Yorkshire agricultural rep. named Tom Umpleby. He had a bit of a dairy round as well, and his wife was a teacher, and together they'd managed to get enough capital together to breed thoroughbreds. Tom was obviously no fool at it, because he had shared Lester's regard for Klairon, and when he'd spotted a late nomination to the stallion for sale at a bargain price, he'd snapped it up. The result of the union was Kithairon.

Eventually Tom and I agreed that I'd take Kithairon back to my yard (I was up north at Middleham then) to see if I could sell him or syndicate him for the £3,000 Tom wanted.

During the ensuing year I discovered that Kithairon looked as though he would amply justify his breeding. I sold a half share to Midlands businessman Jerry Yell, and rang Tom to tell him to expect the cheque. And I said to him, "Keep the other half of the horse, Tom. This will be a good one. He'll win you a lot more than £1,500." Tom was reluctant but he agreed, and I don't think he ever regretted it. Over seven furlongs on soft ground with less than eight stone on his back he became a very hard horse indeed to beat. Tom once told me he'd won more than £17,000 in prize money alone on him.

I won more than that on him. Kithairon became the basis of my stable. To assess any new two-year-old, we only had to run him against Kithairon on the gallops. The Klairon horse was so consistent that we could rate a newcomer down to within a pound or two after a couple of outings with him. More important, Kithairon was for three years an important source of income for me at the start of the season. We would always make certain that he was thoroughly beaten towards the latter part of the previous season, so that he would be lowly weighted in the handicap when the next season started. It was no trouble to produce him for two or three victories early on before his weight was forced back up over the eight stone mark. Even in 1977, after I'd quit and he was being trained by Bill Watts, I was amused to see he won first time out at the bottom of the weights.

Throughout Kithairon's career, however, I was as careful about the placing of his owner as I was about the placing of the horse. If there was a coup in the works I invariably conspired to keep Tom away from the track. Because of his job as a travelling rep. he knew practically every trainer in the north, not to mention countless farmers and tradesmen who were punters, and he'd no sooner get out of his car at the racecourse before he'd be surrounded by his friends asking about his horse's chances. Tom could hardly lie to the people on whom he depended for his daily bread, and down would go the price on Kithairon. So I and Jerry Yell both conspired to keep Tom away, if we could. We were so smart we outsmarted ourselves.

Tom had always seemed more interested in the glory than the gambling and we had run Kithairon in some very fancy company. Tom had been over the moon when he saw his horse run Dragonara Palace to a tight finish in the July Stakes at Newmarket, one of the prestige races of the year, Kithairon had also run some respectable races in superior company at Ascot. But when we sent the horse slumming a bit in order to pull off a gamble against the bookmakers, he didn't appear to be much interested. Of course I always told him in advance when a coup was on, and he'd always thank me for the information, saying, "I might put a little on him down at the betting shop." I figured his yoghurt retailing business could support a fiver each way. Jerry Yell on the other hand would speculate with five thousand. We always spread the money around carefully enough, yet every time we had a coup going the price would shorten on us. I couldn't figure it, until one day during my last year of training I phoned Tom to tell him we had a gamble going. And he said to me, "Well, I'm a bit tied up today, Duke, so would you put down one of my little bets for me at the track?"

"Of course," I said. "Only, what do you mean by one of your little bets?"

"Oh, five hundred."

I nearly fell through the floor. But at last I had an explanation for all the times Kithairon's price fell mysteriously as money came in from off the course.

Getting short-changed on the odds was bad enough. Worst of all was the day at Edinburgh when Tom Umpleby's influence from afar cost me more than £2,000, and cost Jerry Yell even more. Edinburgh's Musselburgh course was as ramshackle a spot from a spectator's point of view as you could find, though it has improved some now. The A1 is so close to the straight that it sometimes looked as though the two-year olds were racing against the lorries for the final furlong. Add to that a perishing wind off the beach and a superb view of the gas works, and it is not exactly a punter's paradise. Still, I daresay few people go there for the scenery. I for one was there that day to pull off a gamble. The race looked like an easy one for Kithairon. Jerry and I had neatly placed our bets far away from the track. All looked rosy on the horizon until I went to see Kithairon in his box.

I was met there by an anxious stable lad. "He's purging somethin' terrible, guv'. It's real diarrhoea." The evidence was scattered powerfully around the box and I immediately sent for the vet. It was a hot day and the vet could find nothing wrong with the rest of his condition.

"They take on a lot of liquid in this weather," he said.

"I think he's just loose. He'll run without coming to any harm."

No harm to the hose, I thought, but how about the harm to his owner and trainer? A horse with bad guts does not win races and we had a lot of money around the country saying Kithairon would win. Quickly I dashed across to the Stewards' room to try to withdraw our entry and save our stakes. However, fast talking and emotional pleading cut little ice against the opinion of the vet as far as the Stewards were concerned and I wasn't allowed to withdraw. They were a dour lot at the best of times, and I left the room with heavy heart. I climbed the steps to the stands with leaden feet and gazed out across the Firth of Forth in the certain knowledge that my two grand was about to be washed out to sea as surely as that litter-laden tide would ebb that afternoon.

Desperately I reached out for crumbs of optimism. Kithairon had a high draw, always a great advantage at Edinburgh. He had a good lad on him. John Curant. And then, unsuperstitious though I was, there was the omen that Kithairon's first win for me was in Scotland; at Ayr, when we'd all collected at 6–1 because Nigel Angus fancied one of his and backed it heavily.

Straws in the wind, all my fancies. They blew away in the first ten seconds out of the start. I could see my gallant steed struggling to give of his best, but he did not have all his strength for the effort. He could do no better than fourth.

For several days afterwards he seemed listless in his box at home, without giving us a clue to what ailed him. Then Ken Mitchard, my head lad, said to me, "I think I know what happened to him, Guv'nor, but I daren't tell you. In fact I think I'll have to go over to the pub and ring you because I don't think I can tell you to your face."

Eventually, upon my promise not to wring his neck or stomp him into the ground, he told me all.

The day before the Edinburgh race he had found Kithairon with traces of a whitish substance around his mouth. There was also a sour smell in the box, but he'd put it down to the hot weather and the horse creating a bit of scum by carrying bits of food into his water. He had seemed perfectly all right.

Then, two days after the disaster, Tom Umpleby had come around on one of his regular visits to the yard. He was a frequent visitor, as was his right, although he took pains to ash my permission first before he went to his horse's box. Tom had walked over to Ken Mitchard and asked him, "Have you seen those two tins I left beside Kithairon's box when I was here the other day, before the race?"

Ken did remember the tins. They'd looked like the kind we used to keep foot greast in. "Yeah, I saw them," he said to Tom. "I threw them out. They'll be up on the tip at Middleham Moor."

"For heaven's sake," said Tom, "they're worth five shillings each!"

"Well, what were they doing there?"

"They had yoghurt in them," said Tom. "Kithairon was brought up on yoghurt from my dairy round. So I brought him a couple of half gallons. He loved it."

Stunned, Ken spelt out for him in words of one syllable exactly how much those two tins of yoghurt had cost me and Jerry Yell. Tom was apologetic, but not terribly impressed. He departed for the rubbish tip to recover his two five-bob containers.

There was little for me to do upon hearing all this but laugh and chalk up another lesson about the Yorkshire soul and eccentric owners. But I made sure Tom reserved his dairy products for his two-legged customers from then on.

CHAPTER ELEVEN

I WAS at the Dublin Sales with Jack Doyle one fine September day, looking for a yearling for one of my owners. I had £4,000 to spend, and was hoping to pick up a good yearling sired by Lavanstell. Jack's aid was invaluable at a yearling sale. He was about fifty years old, but seemed to know everything about every thoroughbred sire and dam over the past century. He'd look at a yearling and tell you, "Ah, lovely little lad. Looks more like his dam than his sire, though." And he'd go on to tell you why the little thing looked more like his mother than his father, and what could be expected from the animal in its racing career.

I did see a yearling I fancied, but noticed it had a big scar on the fetlock of its right hind leg. I asked Jack about it. "That's a good one, Duke, and that scar will never affect its racing. Buy it," he advised.

But I was outbid by a tall, handsome, exceedingly well-dressed black man whom I'd noticed earlier on talking to a friend of mine, Frances Wilby. After the sale she introduced us. His name was Krishna Maharaj, and he said to me, "You know, I'm not sorry I bought that yearling, but I am a bit worried about it. I just discovered he's got a bad scar on his fetlock."

"I know, I saw it before the sale."

"But you bid? You don't think it will stop the horse's racing?"

I laughed. "If I tell you it will stop it, will you sell it to me?"

He grinned. "Does that mean the scar won't stop it?" His voice was crisp and mellow with just a trace of West Indian accent. I learned later that he was a millionaire with origins in Trinidad.

I laughed again. "I'd like to get that yearling from you, but I have to be honest. That scar won't affect it at all."

A week later I was due at the sales in Newmarket, this time selling instead of buying. Robert Sangster had asked me to try to dispose of a yearling for him. It was by Major Portion. Just before I left I got a phone call. "Duke Payne? This is Kris. Krishna Maharaj. Remember?"

I remembered. He said then, "Listen, man, you were so honest with me in Dublin, I want to do something for you. I know you're going to Newmarket. I'll meet you there. You buy a yearling for me and train it. Okay?"

It was okay and then some. I sold Kris the Sangster yearling (it raced as Handsome Major) and he bought himself three others as well. When the day was over he said to me, "Duke, you take all four of them and train them for me."

It was a veritable bonanza. But I had an insuperable problem. "Kris," I said, "I appreciate the offer. I really do. I'm grateful, and I'd love all four of them. But I just don't have the room. I only have a small yard."

"A small yard? A man like you?" He shook his head. We parted company with the understanding I'd just take the Sangster yearling. But the next day a sleek Rolls with KM1 plates pulled into my yard. Out stepped Kris. He came quickly to the point. "Duke, I've been asking around about you, and I like what I hear. You got where you are now by working hard, with nobody to stake you. I started that way. I came over here from Trinidad with not a penny. I started selling yams to make a few shillings. And you know what? I'm still selling yams, only now I'm a rich man. And I want to help you. I think if you had a big place and lots of horses you could be one of the best trainers in the country."

I was more than flattered. I was overwhelmed. But I said to him, "Kris, you're talking very big money. The kind of yard you're talking about is an expensive proposition."

"How expensive?"

"Well, wait a minute, I'll show you. I was just looking at something." I fetched an advertisement I'd clipped out of the paper, more from wishful longing than from any planning. I showed it to him. "This is Berkeley House in Lambourn," I said. "It's gorgeous, and a big place. Ivor Lewis has it, but he's retiring and he wants to sell it."

"What's he want for it?"

"Fifty thousand pounds." This was 1971 money.

Kris nodded. "Where is this place?"

"About fifty, sixty miles from here."

"Good. Get in the car. We'll go right over there and buy it."

It was just about as easy as that. Kris made the deal with Ivor. And he made a deal with me whereby he'd own the place and I'd lease it from him at a low rent. Miracles do happen.

The deal for Berkely House was still kicking around at the solicitor stage when I journeyed to Newmarket again. I was full of myself, not daring to tell anyone yet about my miracle, lest I jinx it back into the real world. By then I had a small family going: Seth the older boy, was two, Joss was one and a bit. I dreamed of how fine they'd grow up on an estate like Berkeley House, and though Lynda and I were not the happiest of couples I hoped that somehow this stroke of fortune would pull us all together.

I was all wrong about those dreams. Though another son was soon to be born to us, Nathan, a son I would lose in tragic circumstances, including legal ones, there is little I can say about me and Lynda except that it didn't work. We each did our separate things, went our separate ways, tied together by the children. I wouldn't leave my boys. Not then. It took a far more disastrous set of circumstances than mere incompatibility to separate me from my boys. But that story is yet to come in this chronicle.

Anyway, I was at Newmarket, and finding myself distracted from the four-legged creatures by a two-legged one. She was an uncommonly beautiful girl and I indulged in the comparison, not for the first time, between comely women and handsome horseflesh. Both horses and women who have that indefinable touch of class walk differently, with an assurance and style that suggests they know what they are on this earth for. They carry their heads high.

Suddenly this girl came up to me and said, "You're Ken Payne, aren't you?" I admitted that I was, and she then asked me my opinion of a horse that was in the ring. I told her what Jack Doyle had told me, that it turned its feet in and would be a doubtful buy.

When the next yearling went into the ring I felt an umbrella poking me in the back of the ribs. I turned around to see an immaculately-dressed gentleman. Oriental, at least in part.

"My secretary tells me you were the one who didn't like that horse I was going to bid for. What do you think of this one?"

"It'll go for a lot of money," I said. "It's by Petingo."

"Bid for me," he said. "Go to £14,000."

Fourteen thousand pounds was not within my credit rating at Newmarket that year, so quickly I collared Jack Doyle to do the bidding. The price went over the limit, but my buyer gave us the nod and we kept going.

The yearling was finally knocked down to Jack at £22,000.

She became Ribotingo. Because of an accident at Ascot as a two-year-old she ran just the one race for me that year. But as a three-year-old she won three times. A dandy little filly she was.

From then on we could hardly stop the man from buying horses. At the end of the day he said to me, "You take them and train them. My secretary will deal with everything. When you get them settled in, come out and visit me."

He walked off without waiting for my reply. I didn't make any objection, just uttered a silent prayer that the Berkeley House closing would be completed in time to accept delivery of all those yearlings. His secretary, that gorgeous thoroughbred whose name was Sue Kennedy, then told me about my benefactor. His name was Eddie Lai, and he was one of the most powerful men in Jamaica. He was a property developer, director of a dozen companies, racing-stable owner and a lot of other things besides.

She also told me that when Eddie Lai asked me to come out and visit him, it was more a polite royal command then an invitation. That, she told me, was the Eddie Lai style. He was a wonderful and generous owner, but if I was to train for him, then I was Eddie Lai's man.

For a couple of halcyon years the Jamaican Connection, as I called it, was paradise. I'd make several trips a year, each lasting two or three weeks, timed to coincide with one of the coups I had planned. I was treated in the grand style. Eddie would pick up the cheque for everything. He'd put me up at the best hotels, usually the Sans Souci at Ocho Rios, where I'd be rubbing elbows with the rich, the film stars, the social elite of several continents.

My timing for these visits was planned to take advantage of the gambling scene as it then was in Jamaica. Most of it was controlled by a Chinese named Liu Shin Chen. There were betting shops by the hundred, back to back, streets of them, particularly in Kingston. The Jamaicans were fast and furious gamblers. They'd bet on anything, even flies crawling up a wall. But they really went overboard for British horse-racing. Because of the time difference, the blowers in the betting shops were going full blast at nine in the morning.

The big thing for me was the odds. There was so much ignorant money flying about that Liu Shin Chen never had to worry about laying off large amounts of it back in Britain to bring the odds down. Neither did he need to indulge in phony morning lines. Whereas in Britain the odds a punter sees in the morning paper are often not the odds he'll get at the betting shop—more on that later—if I saw a horse going at 12–1 in the Jamaican papers, then I'd get 12–1 at the betting shop.

So all I had to do was plan a coup, declare my horse and get him fit, then fly off to Jamaica and back him there. It was beautiful. And with no exchange control regulations. I'd just fill my suitcase with money and bring it home.

I can still remember the air of incredulity with which we pulled it off the first time. It was with a filly named Gay Charmain.

I'd bought Gay Charmain from Phil Solomons, manager of The Batchelors singing group. Phil told me she should have won a number of races but was always left at the start. That didn't bother me. I knew I could get her out flying with careful training. I put her through a process of acclimatisation to the gate on home gallops, raced her against some of my own horses, and she came through with no trouble. Then I entered her in a couple of races at Ripon without punishing her, and as I expected, she lagged behind. She needed a bit more work. We put her through her paces on the gallops again, got her fit and in fine fettle and dropped her into a race at Redcar for the coup.

Two weeks before the race I left for Jamaica. My absence from the course on the day of the race would, I was sure, only help the odds drift out. The bookies would never figure me to pulling off a gamble from four thousand miles away. I checked into the Sans Souci as usual and Eddie sent his big Mercedes around to pick me up. I told him the set-up. He was delighted.

I spent a few days with him looking over his stables, which were at the Caymans Park track. He had an Australian trainer who knew his stuff and I offered no advice unless I was asked. Then we went over to Miami to watch the racing at Hialeah and spend a few days lolling on the beach. The facilities at Hialeah are superb, the course itself gorgeous—flamingoes in residence on an artificial lake; excellent catering facilities; everything laid on for a fun day of racing, win or lose. But the running track itself is tough on the horses, and stories were legion of doping to ease the pain, and of literally standing the animals in buckets of ice before a race to numb their limbs.

I met a few of the American trainers. I got the impression that the "gambling trainer" like myself was the rule, not the exception, in American racing, although the larger purses did help pay the bills.

Back to Jamaica we went. The morning arrived for the big event. I rose, ordered breakfast in my room and phoned England. Gay Charmain would go off around 12–1. I had better than a thousand riding on her. My breakfast came, one of those incomparable Caribbean breakfasts: a pint of fresh lime juice, a slice of papaya, coffee and a proper poached egg, done free in the pan of boiling water.

Breakfast done, I relaxed for a bit in a deck chair, then plunged into the pool for a swim. I did a couple of lengths, climbed out, rubbed myself dry with a rough towel, signalled a waiter and ordered a large Coca Cola with lemon and lots of ice. I knew that at that very monent they'd be off and running at Redcar.

Some ten minutes later came a phone call from Eddie. "No trouble. She trotted in still twelve to one."

I enjoyed another week in the sun, then went home to ponder my next coup. I felt on top of the world. All I had to do was organise winners, which I knew I could do, and get rich backing them in Jamaica at double-figure odds. No more slinking around like a man from MI5, hoping to get a horse at the post at something better than 2–1.

I picked Road Runner for my next Jamaican adventure. I'd sold him to Eddie Lai and nursed him through a few five- and six-furlong races, knowing he needed a mile. When he was ready I put him into a mile seller at Newcastle. Once again I was in swimming costume beside the blue Jamaican waters as my horse came in at 10–1.

Of course it was too good to last. The Jamaicans voted in Mr. Michael Manley and his Leftist government and effectively closed me down. Primarily he put a block on the movement of money out of the country. There was no use in my winning money in Jamaica if I couldn't get it out. I needed the money back home to keep the machine going. Running a big stable cost a fortune. Sadly I returned to the betting wars in Britain.

But Mr. Manley's new regulations did provide me with one last laugh. I saw Liu Shin Chen at Newmarket Sales buying race-horses and yet I knew that the import of bloodstock was another item Mr. Manley had restricted.

When I mentioned it to Chen he said to me, with feigned innocence, "I have not been officially informed of that."

I laughed. "You'll be informed officially soon enough when you try to bring in your horses."

He smiled. "Yes? We will see."

I got the end of the story eventually from Eddie Lai. What Chen did was load his thirty horses on a plane he'd chartered and then made sure his pilot took aboard enough fuel to get to Kingston and no farther. When they got into range of the tower and announced themselves and their cargo, there was a flurry of excitement, then refusal of permission to land.

The pilot told the tower that they had a choice of receiving them either on the tarmac or through the tarmac.

Chen landed his horses. And once landed, he knew how to keep them on the island.

Back on the gambling fields of Britain I was not happy. Lambourn stifled me. The atmosphere was not hospitable for a trainer with the reputation of having a fast gun against the bookmakers. I was also not among those beloved by the Jockey Club. I was anti-Establishment. I was a maverick. Although a number of owners and trainers in the area did make me welcome, to many others I was still a long-haired ex-window cleaner. Worse yet, I had a West Indian partner who sold yams. I was socially unacceptable.

When I'd first moved into Berkeley House I'd gone around to see Sir Hugh Nugent, because permission to use his Mandowne Gallops had not come with the purchase.

I said to him, "You remember me, Sir Hugh? When I was a lad at Atty Persse's yard I once gave you a leg up when you'd fallen off your horse. They called me Duke."

He looked at me closely. "Yes, yes, I remember a lad named Duke. Well, Duke, what brings you back to this valley of hate?"

"Valley of hate?"

"Yes, that's what it is, my boy. There's too much bitterness here. Envy." He shook his head sadly. "Too much envy."

I told him I'd bought Berkeley House.

"Ah," he said, nodding. "You're the window-cleaner chap who bought the place. I heard about it, naturally." He chuckled softly. "And I'll bet they told you I wouldn't let you use my gallops, eh?.'

I smiled. "That's what they told me all right."

He leaned forward and tapped me on the knee. "Well, you just go ahead and use 'em, my boy. You just go ahead and use 'em. And if there's anything else you need you just let my head lad know about it. We'll fix it for you."

He stood up and offered me his hand. "Good luck to you, Duke."

But Sir Hugh had been right about Lambourn. The air was thick with envy, with bitterness, with hate, with social climbing of the most outrageous sort. A year of it was enough for me. In any case. I was doing almost all my racing up north and shuttling the horses back and forth from Lambourn was becoming difficult and expensive. Kris Maharaj agreed we should get out. We sold Berkeley House and bought Kingsley House in Middleham, Yorkshire.

For the four months or so of the flat-racing season Middleham was my headquarters; at other times I operated largely out of the 21 Club in Mayfair, with occasional removals to Bentley's Oyster Bar, Morton's Restaurant and Churchill's Club in Bond Street. With some hundred horses in my stables now, the key part of training was fast becoming the production of owners for my horses rather than winning races. My overheads were tremendous.

Each September there would be a vast new batch of two-year-olds arriving from the studs and the sales rings of Britain and Ireland, with the older horses, too well known for further coups, dispatched all over the globe.

Those two-year-olds had to be found owners and I knew I would not find them among the established wealth that patronised the elite stables of Newmarket and Lambourn. So in the autumn, when the jumpers took over a large part of the racing scene, I returned to the circuit where the famous and the successful met to relax and enjoy themselves.

Through the doors of the 21 Club came a string of people from show business and from the world of trade, men who had made fast money in the boom times of the 'sixties and early 'seventies. The proprietor of the 21, and of Churchill's, Harry Meadows, was a good and loyal friend who owned a few horses himself. I found many of his customers only too pleased to talk about acquiring that ultimate evidence of having "arrived"—a racehorse in training. The promise that in my hands it might even prove a profitable investment was often enough to clinch the deal. The entire atmosphere of the 21 is conducive to the mixing of business and pleasure. It is impeccably run, with excellent food at prices that were high if you were living off your pension, but not excessive for the West End.

The clientelle was invariably in a receptive frame of mind. I recall one manufacturer of electrical appliances, on the town for his wife's birthday, buying her a gift of a race-horse for £1,500. By the following afternoon I had taken them to see it run, and the man won back his purchase price with £500 to spare.

In time, my ability to sell people racehorses became legendary. One night I was out at a boxing match at the International Sporting Club with Billy Shand Kydd and a group of his friends. Billy, son of a wallpaper manufacturing family, had ridden me a winner or two, and he knew my style, on and off the course. We spotted Stanley Baker, the film actor, across the room and someone said to me, "I'll bet you can't sell Stanley a horse. He lives in Epsom and every trainer on the Downs had been up his garden path."

Billy said, "I'll take anyone's £25 that Kenny sells Stanley a horse by the end of the evening."

Billy won his bet with ease. I got myself introduced to Stanley and he volunteered, "I've heard about you. Let's buy a horse for £5,000 or thereabouts and let's see if we can't pull off one good gamble. The bookies have taken me for plenty."

I bought him a horse by Native Prince that he called Rhondda Prince. I set the horse up for a good one at Ayr. He went off at 33–1 and we got beat a short head when the ground turned against us in a sudden downpour. Stanley just said, "Let me know when it's on again." I knew I'd never get 33–1 on Rhondda Prince again, but let it go next at York, and this time we won, on a disqualification. Stanley was delighted. "Do it again, Ken," he said to me. "I love it."

Once more I set up Rhondda Prince for a little coup. This time at Pontefract. How well, and with how much sadness, do I recall the night I phoned Stanley's house to tell him we were coming up again in two day's time, only to learn that Stanley was mortally ill. His wife said to me, "Go ahead with the race, Ken. Stanley would want it."

We won again at Pontefract, but my heart wasn't in it.

The nightclub social scene once cost me dearly. I came out second best in an abortive deal with John Conteh. But I daresay I'm not the only one to be bested by the light heavyweight champion, in and out of the ring. It happened this way.

A man named Roy Salmon approached me one night, and told me he had an anonymous client who was interested in owning a race-horse. I don't know why, but he acted very conspiratorially. He pumped me for information about the economics of horse ownership, then invited me to meet him and his mysterious client the next evening at Trader Vic's Restaurant in the London Hilton.

I was enough of a boxing fan to recognise John Conteh when he walked into Trader Vic's the next night. With him and Salmon was his brother, Tony, who he'd recently appointed as his manager. We chatted for a bit about horses, but by the time the main course arrived it appeared to me that Tony was more interested in betting on winners than he was in acquiring information about owning one. Somewhat coldly I informed him that I was not a tipster. He took the rebuff well enough and over coffee they all agreed to come up to Middleham and continue the conversation.

They duly arrived a couple of days later. John went up and had a look at the gallops, met the lads and had his picture taken with the landlord of The Black Swan in Leyburn. Meanwhile, Tony, Salmon and I fenced around the topic of actually buying a race-horse. By the day's end it was mutually agreed that I should try to buy a couple for them, up to the value of £11,000. We shook hands on the deal.

A couple of weeks later I was with John at the 21 when I got a phone call from Jack Doyle. He told me it was a foul night up at the Newmarket Sales, snow was on the roads and there were few buyers. "You know that Ribocco colt we talked about?" I remembered we had valued it at about £14,000 if it turned out to be anything like its breeding suggested. "Well I got it for two," Jack said.

"Two?" I repeated. I thought I was hearing wrong. "You mean twenty thousand?"

"No, two. Two thousand."

That was one helluva bargain. "Hold on, Jack," I said. I hurried back to my table and told John.

"Great," he said. "See if he can get another one."

Jack came back from Newmarket with another nice young horse and we still had spent only £5,000 of the £11,000 the Conteh brothers had authorised. But after a couple of weeks the auctioneers needed paying. I asked for something on account. I was told the money would be forthcoming, but meanwhile would I try to get one more horse for the remaining £6,000? I went down to Newmarket myself and bought the Contehs their third horse. Though no money had as yet arrived we had shaken hands on the deal and I wasn't worried.

Then, one evening when I was with John at the 21 Club, we decided to go over to Churchill's. When we walked in the cabaret was just starting and we got the four star treatment, including an affectionate joke or two from the comedian. Afterwards came one of the Churchill's oldest institutions—the horse-race. They have three wooden horses on the stage, complete with saddles and bridles and even a whip. The idea is to progress across the stage in a kind of parody of the rocking horse winner. Customers from the audience are invited to take part. It's all good clean fun; the management hands out gold cuff-links or small gifts for prizes and the participants depart to a healthy round of applause. I had taken part many times as Churchill's "house" jockey.

On this particular evening John and I were invited up, and we climbed into the saddles for the "off".

John seemed to be in high good humour, although he couldn't get the hang of his wooden horse. He laughed as the odd rocking motion of the horse threw him about. As we came across the stage for the finish the unthinkable occurred—the champion fell off.

There were roars of laughter and a slightly strained smile from John. Little did I know how much that fall from a wooden horse would cost me.

A few days later I got a message to call Tony Conteh. I rang him, and he said to me, without preliminaries, "I've decided we don't want to go through with the deal."

I was shattered. "Look," I said, "I've got £11,000-worth of race-horses I'm committed to paying for on your behalf."

"Well, that's your decision," he said.

"And John goes along with that?" I asked.

"That's right."

"I'd like to hear that from John himself," I insisted. "I want John to tell me to my face that the deal is off."

"Okay, we'll meet you," said Tony. "How about the Euston Station buffet?"

I could hardly believe my ears. "I'm willing to meet you almost anywhere," I replied. "I'll even pay for the drinks. But I'm not going to discuss this business in a railway cafe."

Finally we agreed to meet at the Holiday Inn near Marble Arch. There John confirmed his brother's words. He mumbled something about being humiliated by the incident of the horse-race at Churchill's.

I'll give him this much; he seemed damned embarrassed about what he was saying to me.

I didn't bellyache to anyone, but word got around. Two days later Harry Meadows asked me if I was in the hole for the eleven grand. I had to admit I didn't have the cash to pay the auctioneers. "Don't worry, I'll see what I can do," he said. In short order he got a few friends around, including Max Bygraves and his manager Jock Jacobson, and they took care of the most expensive horse. That was a big help, but at the end of the day I was still out of pocket quite a few thousand.

On a lighter note, the social sensitivity of another of my owners cost me a horse not long after the Conteh affair. I bought a two-year-old for Don Ward, who owned a strip club in Soho called the New Sunset Strip. He called the horse New Sunset, and after getting the animal ready I entered it for a six-furlong sprint. Quite naturally Don saw an easy chance for some publicity in the tabloids. He suggested sending a few of his girls up to Middleham to pose with New Sunset, wearing little more than the horse usually did. I didn't mind, it was a fun idea and if it did Don's club a little good, why not? I fixed a date with Don for a week hence. He would lay on the photographers.

But then Thelma Wade called me. Thelma was one of my more important owners, and she didn't like the idea of strippers posing with a Ken Payne horse at Middleham. It would lower the tone, not only of my establishment but of all the other owners who had horses with me. It wouldn't do at all. She was genuinely furious. I couldn't afford to offend her. She'd been too good to me. I had to phone Don and tell him the publicity stunt was off. Middleham never saw the strippers, and I never saw any more of the horse.

I suppose Thelma was not all wrong, although at the time I certainly thought she was being a bit blue-stockinged about a harmless publicity gimmick. She did have her image to protect, and important friends who might well have thought the photo in questionable taste. And, since the two of us were closely associated, it could have proved embarrassing for her.

She was living then in considerable splendour at Sutton Courtenay in the house Sir Michael Sobell used to own. The place was resplendent with swimming pool, sauna, salons, sculptured gardens and dozens of bedrooms. She entertained lavishly, and the newspapers were filled with tales of parties at Sutton Courtenay, parties glittering with beautiful girls, film stars and Arab sheikhs. Thelma wasn't averse to publicity, as long as it was the right kind.

In a way we were two of a kind and her house sometimes reminded me of my own Kingsley House—there always seemed to be somebody hanging around who wanted paying. But Thelma was a resourceful girl, who thought nothing of hopping on a plane to the Gulf and prevailing upon one of her Arab friends if there was a temporary difficulty to overcome.

She'd come a long way for a Yorkshire lass who started out as a student nurse. She married an extremely capable young general practitioner and she was determined from the first that they'd move up in the world. She saw a house available in Harley Street and took it. Within a year or so the Wades, with Thelma as the business brain, had a thriving, fashionable practice. Each year at Christmas she threw a fabulous party and at the end of one I even persuaded the man who did the catering, Peter Jaeger, to buy race-horses. The wide circle of monied friends to whom she introduced me did a lot to get me off the ground as a major trainer of flat-race horses.

She herself had taken up racing in style once I'd beguiled her into owning her first horse. The night I first met her, which was the night I brought George Pantin home to Maidenhead where she then lived, she said to me, "I wouldn't mind owning a race-horse, but it would have to be as black as it could be." A lot of horses had gone under the wire when I next phoned her, perhaps two years later. She remembered me at once, and asked me why I'd never bought her a horse.

"I've got one for you now," I said. It was a horse called Anubis. Later I added another black one to her string, Amenhotep. Thelma liked a gamble, and though she ran lavish receptions at Ascot for the injured jockeys' fund and became a notable figure at the smarter tracks, she loved the little coups we slipped in at the less glamorous courses.

She went down to Lingfield with me the first time we pulled off a coup with Amenhotep. We went by train that day, with Frank Morby, who I had engaged to ride the horse. Or at least I thought I'd engaged him. But when we got to the track Thelma said to me, "Something's wrong, Ken. According to the form-book, Frank Morby's riding Zaffer, the favourite."

I scurried around to the paddocks. I couldn't find Frank, who obviously was avoiding me. But I collared my travelling head lad and asked him who was riding Amenhotep. "Geoff Baxter, guv'."

"What do you mean, Geoff Baxter? Morby's supposed to be riding!"

"That's what I thought when we got here, guv', but then I found he was riding Zaffer. So I got Baxter instead. And lucky I was that he was available, too."

I had no quarrel with that. Baxter was a capable rider. But Morby knew the horse. To this day, I won't know why Frank travelled all the way down on the train with me, and didn't tell me that he had taken on another horse.

Be that as it may, we had our money down off the track and were committed. Just before the race it began to pour with rain. Thelma asked, "Is it good for us or bad for us, this rain?" I didn't feel like giving her my answer to that.

The horses were launched from the gate in a sea of mud. And lo and behold—Baxter beat Morby to the wire. I couldn't believe my luck. I had five hundred going for me each way at 12–1. For once justice triumphed for Ken Payne.

That race was on a Thursday, and in celebration Thelma threw one of her celebrated wingding weekend parties. In any case, win a race or lose, there was a weekend party going at Thelma's place. I didn't make them all, but I made most of them. I also made a few special friends among the people who were regulars at Sutton Courtenay for weekends. Notable among them was a girl named Jackie Hartman, who owned an art gallery on

Duke Street. Jackie turned me on to the world of art and to trying my own hand at painting. I'm still interested and I still paint. I'm no Stubbs, but I have been told that my racing scenes and my horses are not all that bad.

By 1975, although Thelma was still going strong, I was aware that the recession was pinching. It has already picked off a few of my owners. Kris Maharaj had taken a terrible beating in property. Just after New Year's Day, Thelma happened to mention to me that the school fees for her children were coming due. She wasn't hinting, just groaning aloud as so many people were at the time.

"Hang on a few months, Thelma," I told her. "When the flat season starts we'll both be back in the money."

The source of my confidence was one of Thelma's little dark fillies named Shukrun. She had been showing up well on the gallops and had no record to show for the bookmakers. But I intended taking no chances. In the interval I put her on a course of B-12 and steroids so that she'd be well muscled and mature for the early racing. She was tried against two of our best work-horses, and then galloped twice at Ripon. She was ready for a walk-up at five furlongs.

The coup was set for Doncaster. The night before, I stayed at Sutton Courtenay. I rose early, since it was a fair drive to Doncaster and I wanted to get there well in time to saddle up and talk to my iockey. I climbed into my E-type and spun down the gravel drive to the big iron gates. Then I realised I'd forgotten the little electronic box you needed to open them. I turned around and zipped back to the house. I went up the stairs to my bed-room, where I'd left the box. As I passed the bathroom I could hear the sound of water running. Figuring Thelma was in the bath I didn't bother to call out that I'd returned.

The phone rang and I picked it up. A voice said, "Has he gone yet?"

Something made me say, "Who, Ken?"

"Yes. Does he say it'll win?"

I recognised the voice; it belonged to a man from Ladbroke's I'd met once at a weekend party.

Silently I put the phone down. I grabbed the gate buzzer and hurried out.

On the drive up the M1 and across to Doncaster I had plenty of time to think, plenty of time to worry. After a long, lean winter I was in need of a handsome coup. If the overnight odds of 8–1 on Shukrun stayed there for the start I could win about £21,000, enough to keep Lloyds Bank at Catterick at bay for a few weeks, or at least until the flat season was well under way. For me, April ushered in open season on bookies.

But if that phone call meant what I thought, then I was in for some unpleasant news at Doncaster.

I parked, and walked straight around past the imposing new stand. One glance at the boards told me the story. Shukrun was the favourite, and showing 3–1. Even 2–1 in some places.

I went into a phone box and called Peter Gold. Peter was one of my owners. He was also a very high-stake gambler and a very special friend. When I got through to him he said, "Some secret, that filly of yours. Three blondes have been backing it all over London since half past ten this morning."

I put the phone down and called the Stallion Brothers, the bookmakers. "We've had fortunes for her," came the terse report.

I could see ten or twelve thousand pounds profit disappearing before my eyes. It never even crossed my mind that Shukrun might not win. This was one of those cast-iron certainties. The trouble was, the whole world seemed to know it.

I wandered back down towards the rails where the crowds were starting to gather around the bookmakers. I noticed that not many punters were taking the odds on

Shukrun. It was painfully obvious that the money was coming in heavily from off the course. Then Danny Hanahan strolled up to me. A huge, rollicking man, I'd once trained for him before the stress of dealing not only with Danny but with his endless stream of brothers, Mo, Lou, John and Big John, got the better of me and we called it quits.

"Beat you today, Kenny," he said to me, slapping me on the back. "We'll trot up."

Danny had a horse called Mister Jim running in the same race as Shukrun. His beast didn't have a chance. But I seized the opportunity to use Mister Jim in a desperate gamble to save what was left of my coup. It was obvious that either by accident or by design, or because she simply couldn't resist the cachet of being "in the know", Thelma had blown our secret. There was only one way I could possibly rectify the error.

Quickly I walked back to the rails, and started taking any price I could get on Danny Hanahan's horse. In two minutes I had staked better than £2,000 on Mister Jim. It was a calculated gamble. I had deliberately to lose the two grand in order to shift the odds on Shukrun enough to more than make up for that loss. The bookmakers, normally so swift to cut a price when "hot money" comes in, seemed painfully slow to react. Then, slowly, the odds on Shukrun began to drift out—to 4–1, then 5–1. There they stuck. I would be a couple of thousand to the good, anyway.

Just before post time, Thelma herself arrived—in somebody else's Rolls Royce. I felt bitterly disappointed in her.

The race itself was a formality. Shukrun coasted home.

At the auction afterwards, Mick Easterby came in to bid strongly for the filly. For once I was indifferent to seeing the price being driven up. I went with him for a bit and then dropped out, leaving him with a good animal, but no bargain.

I picked up the slip of paper from the auctioneers and went to see the woman with whom, over the years, I had shared more than the usual thrills and vicissitudes of racing.

Thelma was having a drink and chatting as gaily as ever. I gave her the sale note. "You no longer have a horse," I said to her. "And as of now, you no longer have a trainer."

CHAPTER TWELVE

I NEVER claimed to be anything other than what I was—a gambling trainer. I was good at it, thoroughly professional at it, for a time the best there was. I had to arrange the races for my horses so carefully that only the sinister hand of Fate itself could keep me from the winner's enclosure. Of course the best-laid plans of mice and men, etc.; I did get beaten now and again. I wasn't the only trainer manipulating horses and races. And even the legendary Man o' War got beaten once, when thoroughly caged in by other horses.

But I won a lot more often than I lost. And I won at the longest odds I could possibly fix. There was no point in picking up a string of £500 purses and the glory of being the leading trainer in the North. They wouldn't buy enough to pay for the hay, much less feed all the other hungry mouths I had around my Middleham stables.

I don't think I ever did anything illegal, but I confess I worked damned hard to screen my intentions from the bookmakers. There are, after all, lots of ways to stop a horse legally. All you need as a textbook is a set of Dick Francis novels. You can leave him thirsty and then give him the classic bucket of water before he runs. Who knows how often that is done? You can also have the horse shod with heavy plates. It's amazing how many horses you see walking around parade rings with clumsy work-shoes on. Admittedly, many of these come from mean trainers who are just trying to turn an extra penny by charging owners for plates and blacksmith's services without actually using them. Deliberate or not, the effect is the same; there is no way a horse with work plates is going to win a race.

Ghoulishly, you can even draw blood. I've never used this Dracula technique to slow a horse; on the contrary, I've used it to win a race. By bleeding a horse then transfusing back a couple of pints before a race you give the horse extra oomph.

In the extreme case, if a trainer thinks his horse may escape from an inexperienced jockey, he can tranquilise him—the horse, that is. That's a risky business, and can show up in the dope test. Only once to my knowledge has it ever been done and it's something I would never do. It's just not necessary. The most common ploy with younger horses is to keep them untrained to stalls so they are left at the start. A slow start can also be arranged by any good jockey. To be as generous as possible to my former colleagues, I would say that at least ten per cent of the slow starts you see are deliberate. A horse can give away weight, he can sometimes beat a bad draw, but it is well-nigh impossible to recover the distance lost in a really bad start.

My own favourite techniques were the simplest. If I was not too keen on a horse winning a race I would use methods that are perfectly permissible within the rules of racing, yet often go unnoticed by the racing professionals, let alone the betting public. I'd either run him out of his distance or over ground that did not suit him. Even Grundy took a pasting from Mark Antony when the Newbury ground was against him, and most horses are fastidious to the point of rebelliousness about ground they don't like.

Perhaps even more important was distance, which was not always the one suggested by a horse's breeding. For example, though Constable was the sharpest of sprinters, he never begot a sprinter in his stud career; yet he bred some splendid milers and mile-and-a-quarter winners. Indigenous, which burnt up the Ascot track to become the fastest race-horse in the world, bred three- and four-mile 'chasers and hurdle winners.

Once I got to know a horse's ideal distance, it was a simple matter to run him out of it when I wanted to set up a string of zeroes before his name in the form book. Then I'd drop him back in to pull off the coup. Sometimes weights, and the condition of the track, would lengthen or shorten the horse's ideal distance, and he could win a furlong more or less either way, but not much more than that. Rare indeed is the six-furlong sprinter which can win at a mile, and vice versa.

This would seem to be so obvious that I was amazed to get away with it for so many years. I suppose the answer is that even the so-called professionals do not chart form as closely as they should. And the average punter can't always find the information he needs to make an intelligent bet, even if he knows what to look for. I wouldn't like to say that the average punter is a mug. But he does let trainers like me, and the bookies, make a mug of him.

The misguided punter is the one who believes that every horse in a race has a chance to win, that every horse is sent out to win every time he races, or, at least, is in shape to win. Conversely, the misguided punter will believe that because a horse loses three or four races in a row he's a rotten horse and should be avoided. As the song says, it ain't necessarily so. A serious punter should study his trainers as well as his horses, and know which trainers are gambling trainers. He should know a horse's best weight, ground and distance. Unfortunately, punters do not arm themselves with this information. I say unfortunately now; when I was training and gambling I would have had to say fortunately.

As for betting on maiden races, a punter might as well blindfold himself and stick a pin in the starting list. Unless he has more information than is generally published about maidens, he can't have a clue about a trainer's intentions. The professional tipsters in the newspapers can sometimes help, but obviously a trainer like me would make sure no journalist ever knew what he was planning.

When a new horse arrived at my yard, I began by getting him fit. A lot of completely spurious mystique surrounds trainers' methods of getting horses ready: the exact number of inches of road work they do, what time they get out in the morning, the stop watches on the gallops, and so forth.

I'll reveal my secret: by and large horses get themselves fit.

If they are fed on the best, given proper graduated exercises and looked after by skilled and careful stable staff, they will be fine. Once they are wind fit and not blowing at the end of a gallop they are ready.

I would then try them against one of the senior horses that I already knew. I always had a couple of animals which were absolutely genuine and true; I knew what they could do down to the last pound in weight. Kithairon and Porcupine Pie were like that. So I would take a new horse and run him against Kithairon, for example, with Kithairon carrying perhaps a stone more in weight. If the new horse could stay with Kithairon over three or four furlongs I'd gradually reduce Kithairon's weights until I knew exactly what the novice could do. And aside from myself only my head lead, Ken Mitchard, would know how much weight the lead horse was carrying on any given day.

That was about all the time I'd need to spend on the gallops. The rest of the time the lads were able to take care of the training.

Unless I was second-guessing the bookies in a maiden

race, I would not expect a novice horse to win the first couple of times out. Even I was chary of trying a coup in a maiden race, although I have done it. Who could know the worth of the other maidens in the race? And who could tell what lunacy some unschooled maiden might get up to when the pack headed for the rails? A dangerous business, betting maiden races. But just to help camouflage a ready maiden, I'd run the animal out of its distances or send it to the course without giving it any schooling in stalls.

In any case a horse's first race can be traumatic. During the running of the race there is an eerie kind of silence over the pack . . . the only sounds are the blowing of the horses, the creaking of leather and the groans and curses of the jockeys. Then suddenly the horses hit the area of the stands, and the noise of the crowd comes like a thunderclap. The novice horse may become unnerved, hesitate, break stride. Its speed will drop abruptly, and the other horses will pass it before it can recover.

All this is quite apart from the Tannoy and the general noise and confusion at a track that can make a horse nervous. My horses always looked well in the paddock and often got the lads the award for the best turned-out horse, but I never believed in elaborate plaiting and grooming which simply got the animal over-excited too soon before its time to race. Horses know they're in competition, and different horses react differently to the knowledge of a coming race. As my old mentor Atty Persse used to say, horses have a way of telling you things, if you'll only take the time to listen.

Control of the horse's condition and the race in which he was entered, those were the vital things in planning a coup. But if I felt there was still some danger that an animal might do something daft and win when it was supposed to lose, I would resort to giving the jockey wrong orders. As I've said, I've never told a jockey to hook up a horse. But I might tell him to hold him back when I knew the horse was a front runner, or take him wide when I knew the horse liked to go with the bunch.

All this was in the ideal world when you had an owner like Stanley Baker or Peter Gold, who could afford to nurse a horse for one big coup; all too many of my owners were like myself, in need of some cash tomorrow, or preferably yesterday.

It was with a Peter Gold horse that I had one of my disasters, despite the most careful planning. He had bought a yearling which he called Sling Wrap, and as soon as we had him out for his first spin on Middleham Moor I knew we had a winner. He was genuine. He knew what his business was. Throughout his time as a two-year-old we nursed him for one big gamble the following year. I ran him a couple of times on the wrong ground and when he was not fully fit. He showed nothing except that he was very fast out of the stalls, because we were putting some intensive education into him back home on this vital subject.

Through the winter he got the full treatment; B-12, steroids, the works. Then I took him down privately to Ripon for a gallop with a number of other horses. Ripon was no distance from Middleham and the management was very kind to me and let me gallop there. Sling Wrap made mincemeat of his colleagues and I knew he was ready.

He was entered for a mediocre evening meeting at Newcastle. I studied the declared runners, but even then I didn't decide to run him until I saw that he had an acceptable, if not perfect, draw. He had a good handicap but I decided to gild the lily by putting apprentice Stan Eccles on him, to claim another seven pounds. In addition, I knew that by putting Eccles up I'd convince the bookies that Sling Wrap was not intended to win. Yet I knew Eccles could handle the assignment. I'd sent him out fifty or sixty times on horses I knew couldn't win, and he had shown that he could ride to orders, handle a big, strong horse, and could keep his head during a hard race.

Peter Gold is also a cool one, one of the coolest gamblers I've ever known. And one of the biggest. I've seen him in the Curzon Club helping our balance of payments no end by trouncing overseas visitors at baccarat and staking thousands on the turn of a card at poker. From his immaculate town house in Oxford Square fortunes are redistributed over the racecourses of Western Europe. Heaven only knows how much he had down on Sling Wrap that night. I'd managed to get £500 on for myself at 4–1, via the betting shops. By the time the horses were going to the post I had another £1,500 on and the way the odds were falling on Sling Wrap it was obvious to the multitude that another Ken Payne coup was in the works. I couldn't always keep the odds long in my battles with the bookies.

But I was getting bad vibrations. Sling Wrap was going in one of the later races and already there had been two enquiries that night. One had been utterly ridiculous. The third horse, which had finished nine lengths behind, had been given the race, with the first two placed last. The crowd had gone wild and I knew that with decisions like that coming from the stewards, anything might happen. I've always thought the stewards at Newcastle would be more gainfully employed looking after the wildlife sanctuary or the caravan park next door. But we had to live with them.

The light was already fading a bit when they went off, and it was hard to make out what was happening as they came level with Gosforth Lake. But as I picked them up I could see that Sling Wrap was going well. Unfortunately it was all too clear that one of Arthur Stephenson's horses was also going well. I swore softly. Arthur is one of those racing men, like Les Hall, Denys Smith and Geoff Tofts, you always have to fear. He's not only a skilled trainer but a very clever placer of horses. If one of his was trying, then we were going to have a hard time of it.

Coming into the final furlong Sling Wrap was behind but well placed. A gap opened up on the rails and closed fast but it was enough for Eccles to push Sling Wrap through. They fought out a close finish over the last fifty yards and Eccles got him home by a neck. But I knew that would not be the end of it. As we were leading the horses in, the stewards were announcing the third enquiry of the evening. On the way over I met Arthur Stephenson. He has always been a gentleman, an honest and generous man, a relentless rival you can enjoy competing against. He clapped me on the shoulder. "You have a lot on?"

"A fair bit."

"Well, I know it means a lot more to you than it does to me," he said. "We'll just have to see how lucky we can be. After all, your boy did win."

We went in to see the gentlemen who were to decide the fate of an awful lot of money. One of them said to me, "Well, Payne, what did you think of the riding of your boy?"

"Obviously the gap was closing," I replied. "The other boy didn't have to stop riding and they fought out a good fair finish."

"Stephenson?" I knew the Newcastle stewards had had a few brushes with him, too.

"What can you say?" shrugged Arthur. "They're little boys riding big horses. As they get to the end the horses are tiring. They tend to wander. I thought it was six of one, half a dozen of the other.

As soon as Arthur finished we were told to get out. A minute later we were called back in.

"Stephenson, your horse gets the race. Payne's horse is placed last."

It was obvious to me that they knew a gamble had been pulled off and I figured it was their way to teach Ken Payne a lesson. I also believe that Arthur's acceptance of my win outraged them; had he fought belligerently to get my horse disqualified the stewards might well have given me the race. But that's hindsight.

However, the punters were less than amused at the ruling. There were shouts, catcalls, shaking fists, the stands had to be cleared for a bomb threat and the rest of the evening's racing was disrupted. None of which got me or Peter Gold our money back.

Fortunately I did not often give the stewards a chance to interfere in my execution of a coup. And I usually had two or three horses in my yard which were insurance policies against disaster. One was a beautiful black midget I bought as a yearling at Newmarket Sales. He was laughably tiny throughout his life, yet he was to turn into a walking textbook of my approach to racing.

The day after I bought him, though, he wasn't walking at all. As we were unloading him, he slipped, and broke a bone in his leg. It was certain that he should be put down, but the insurance company sent a cat-and-dog vet out to look at him. He inspected the break, saw that the colt could take some weight on the foot, and refused to let us shoot him. He said the animal might well come right again. Either way I was £1,500 in the hole. If I put him down privately—it was clear he was in some pain—the insurance company would not pay out. On the other hand, I couldn't see him ever racing.

We put him on deep litter and he went to skin and bone. But finally he could hack around on all four legs and I let him go for £300 to Tommy Mansfield, the barrow boy, as a pony for the kids. And I forgot about the little yearling colt.

A couple of years later I was on a return trip to old haunts—and in fact, old company—for the meeting at

Windsor. For once, even on the racecourse, I was beguiled by the beautiful young lady I was with and not paying too much attention to the horses. Suddenly she pointed on to the track where the horses were parading. "I want to back that one," she said. The horse she fancied was a beautiful little black creature, shiny as a new apple, running under the name of Say Jade and trained by Arthur Goodwill at Newmarket. I recognised the breeding, and sure enough it was owned by Tommy Mansfield. My little black calamity had actually made it to the race track.

I had drifted apart from Tommy Mansfield during the passing two years. I think it was because he thought I was leaving him out of bets. Actually this was true. But I'd stopped informing him because it had seemed to me that he wanted information just to pass on to his shop staff. I was never greedy, but spreading the word around to all and sundry was a sure-fire way to send the odds plummeting like a barometer in a hurricane. Unlike me, all Tommy had to do to make extra money was raise the price of his apples. I depended on odds.

Anyway, I looked down at that tiny creature going to the post at Windsor with more than passing interest. I figured it owed me £1,200.

The race was for maidens over a mile and a quarter. Say Jade was left a bit at the post and finished well behind the pack. Naturally enough, the sporting press next day had little to say about him. Fortunately, for me at least, there were not many eyes in racing to see what there was to be seen. For during the running of the race Say Jade had shown something remarkable. Coming off the bad start he'd caught the field and gone clear at seven furlongs before fading badly. It was quite a performance, if you were prepared to evaluate it properly. I was. But I said nothing and went home.

Next week I looked in the paper, and there he was

again, declared for another race at Windsor at the same distance in good company. I flew down especially to see him run, along this time, with no distractions. In the paddock I had a look at his leg; sure enough, the lump was still there. The race itself proved to be the same story, more or less. He got off to a better start this time, made the running for seven furlongs, then disappeared from sight. But I knew my original judgment had been right: this was a race-horse. Only his distance was seven furlongs; not the mile or more his breeding suggested.

After the race I made sure to bump into Tommy Mansfield. "I see you've still got that little black pony I sold you. I thought he was for your kids?"

"Yeah, that's how I should have left him," Tommy said. "I'm not going to run him again. Fiddler says he's no good and he'll never make anything." Arthur Goodwill is known as "Fiddler" in tribute to his talents on the violin rather than for any tricks on the racecourse.

"That little horse owes me £1,200," I said to Tommy, "never mind the air fare down on British Midland to watch him run today. Listen, you've been saying you want a gamble. Well okay, that's a horse that could do both of us a world of good. You get Arthur to run him again."

A horse carries top weight the first three times he runs. Then he's handicapped; usually, if he performs as badly as Say Jade, to a considerably lower weight. I wanted this horse handicapped under the care of Arthur Goodwill. By then nobody in the British Isles would have taken any notice of that sort of form from a Kenny Payne horse.

Say Jade ran again for Arthur, with the same result, over the same distance. Tommy said, "I'm taking him home, Duke. Fiddler says he's just no good."

I said to Tommy, "Turn him out. Make sure he gets plenty of good grub and let me have him during the winter."

A couple of months later, when I drove through the gates of Kingsley House, I was met by my head lad. "What have you done, guv'nor?" he said. "We've got too many horses already, even back of the pub, and you go and do this?"

"What are you talking about?"

"This afternoon," he said, "this guy rolls up to the place with one of them little pig-trailers attached to his out crawls this thing. I would have sent it back except the man kept saying Ken promised this and Ken promised that. Take a look for yourself. It can't hardly see over the top of the box."

I laughed. "Don't you worry about it," I said. "It'll earn its keep."

A couple of mornings later Say Jade went out for a gallop with Tommy Lappin aboard.

Tommy was another "find", my best jockey. When I'd first arrived at Kingsley House I'd needed some brick-laying done. I'd asked my neighbour, Capt. Neville Crump, if he could recommend anyone to me.

"There's a chap called Lappin who could do it. But he's better at riding horses than he is at laying bricks."

The name had jogged my memory. Lester Piggott had mentioned a Tommy Lappin when he'd heard I was moving up north. In his usual deadpan fashion Lester had told me, "Used to be a good apprentice up there. Lappin. Don't know what happened to him."

That was enough endorsement for me. Tommy Lappin, brick-layer, became my number one jockey. He had been out of the game through a row with his old boss, but to me he showed some qualities rare in a jockey. He could not only ride to orders, but afterwards he could tell you what every horse in the race had been doing, including the six who hadn't been trying. Above all, he had the ability to get the very best out of a horse and give you an exact assessment of its true potential. I came to rely on Tommy's judgment on the course and off it, second only to Ken Mitchard, my head lad.

Tommy had been among the sceptics when he'd first laid eyes on Say Jade. But it had taken just a week to convince him. Soon he had the colt running over the gallops with our best and from the very beginning we saw something beautiful in the creature: he knew only one thing—to run his heart out.

Yes, Say Jade was that most precious of animals, an utterly genuine racehorse which would unstintingly do the best it could, every time. When you train horses over the years you see, amongst your own and amongst other strings, high-class horses which seem to lack courage or the will to win. Marinsky comes to mind. Such horses are the despair of their connections. But a horse like Say Jade was a joy to train, because every bit of his little heart was in the business of racing.

I groomed him as one of our guaranteed meal-tickets for the coming season. He got his full measure of tender loving care, plus the full course of the System: drenching, blood count, vitamins iron and steroids. At the start of the season we put him in a seller at Catterick. He was in much cheaper company and carrying his low handicap weight but there was no chance of his winning. I made sure he was a couple of gallops short of being wind fit and at six furlongs he was caught short on distance. Besides, Catterick is such a sharp track that its six furlongs is the equivalent of only five anywhere else. Tommy Lappin rode and he was comfortably beaten without the stewards being upset or the bookmakers getting suspicious.

We took him home and galloped him against Kithairon, our most reliable trial horse, until we knew down to the last pound what he would do. We got him wind fit, and now he was ready for the coup.

I declared him for a seven furlong seller at Redcar. You could have put the Crown Jewels on him and slept soundly. He trotted up, and I won £7,000.

Next time out I raced him at a mile. He was the hot favourite, and he was beaten, as I knew he would be. He was a seven-furlong horse, not six and not eight.

I had to be careful with a good horse like Say Jade. I couldn't get greedy and take another bite of the apple too soon. Odds would not be long enough, and I could arouse the ire of the stewards. On the other hand, the handful of horses in which I had total confidence were my sole reliable source of ready cash, training fees being a sporadic and erratic means of paying the wages and the other bills. Inevitably there came cash crises. One week when the till was looking a bit anaemic I had to wheel Say Jade out again.

It was a seller up at Hamilton, and I knew the odds would be shorter than the Italian Register of War Heroes. But I was in a bind. I knew I could get on with a bookmaker at the course, but in the event I had to lay out £700 to try to win £1,200.

Considering its proximity to Glasgow, Hamilton is rather an attractive little track. And from the stands I had a beautiful view of the horror story that was to follow. It was an old-fashioned barrier start which duly attracted all those sulky animals which had refused to co-operate with stalls elsewhere. There was a lot of milling about and considerable delay. It seemed to me as though the starter deliberately chose the precise moment when there was maximum confusion to hit the barrier handle and let them go.

John Curant was on Say Jade and I could see all too clearly a horse with Tommy Mansfield's colours standing with its back to the barrier having a nibble at the trees while the rest of the field was on its way. Curant should have stood still, but he turned Say Jade around and set off, hopelessly behind.

When I saw my bookmaker a few moments later he was

laughing his head off. "You want to pay me now or will you settle with me tomorrow at Redcar?" he said.

Paying him then and there was out of the question. But I didn't understand his reference to Redcar. "Why Redcar?" I asked him. "I haven't got any runners there tomorrow."

"Sure you have. I saw your name in the evening paper. I don't remember the horse, though."

I remembered. It suddenly came back to me that I'd declared Say Jade for Redcar, a bit brutally, though out of necessity, figuring that if he had an easy time of it at Hamilton I might just have another go the next day and outwit the bookies. "Let me see the paper," I said to the bookie. I checked out the entries with Say Jade, told the bookie I'd see him at Redcar and went over to my traveling head lad. "How is he?" I asked.

"He's fine. Bad luck, guv'."

"Okay," I said. "Cool him off. Give him some good feed and let him rest in his box till four o'clock tomorrow morning. Then get him over to Redcar for the first race."

I went back to the bookmaker. "Say Jade is four to one in the papers for tomorrow. Will you take a bet on him now?"

"You're going to run that horse again tomorrow at Redcar? You must be crazy."

"So take my bet, then."

He looked at me suspiciously. "How much?"

"Five hundred."

"Okay. But only to win."

I stayed in Glasgow the night. I did not sleep easily. There were hazards at Redcar for the unwary. The running rail was not absolutely straight, there was at least one patch of false ground that might have been specially imported from the beach, and you could never be sure where you were in the draw, as the stewards were liable to move the stalls from one side of the course to the other.

All that was aside from the risk I was taking running Say Jade two days in a row. But I was short of cash and now into the bookie for £1,200. When I awoke early the next morning I was a shambles, but still with the gut feeling that my little colt would pull me out of the hole. I made a few phone calls and spread another thousand around on him. What the hell, in for a penny in for a pound. I felt better for demonstrating the courage of my convictions. Some would have called it sending good money after bad.

When I got to Redcar I looked Say Jade over. He still seemed to be jumping out of his skin, as handsome a little devil as ever. Then I briefed Curant as carefully as possible. He was a very strong jockey with a ferocious finish, but even in my present straits I did not want him knocking Say Jade about. Then I retired to the stands, which were still filling up for the first race.

This time there was no nonsense about barriers. Say Jade fairly flew out of the stalls. Two furlongs out he was cruising and I knew the bills would be paid until the next time. He won with a couple of lengths in hand and my bookmaker friend was not laughing as he handed over the £800 he owed me. I stayed to give Say Jade a pat and then took off past the great chemical works and rolling-mills of Teeside back to Middleham and a respite from the more frantic demands of the banks.

Say Jade won a couple more times for me, and then his old leg injury began to play him up. He had been a good friend to me, so I let him go to a pony stud in the New Forest at Ringwood, where they wanted to bring in some thoroughbred blood. It is a beautiful run place, like a mini version of the National Stud.

I told Tommy Mansfield that he would never be abused. And he never has been.

CHAPTER THIRTEEN

FLEECING the bookmakers, that was the name of the game. Taking their money in order to keep my stables going was more than just a necessity for me, it was entertainment. I loved it. The big bookmakers were the enemy and for my money they are a plague on British racing.

Bookmakers take millions out of British racing to buy properties, build hotels, open bingo halls and leisure centres. They operate in a manner which should make them daily targets of the Trade Descriptions Act, offering prices in the papers that you rarely get. You can ring up at nine-thirty in the morning and ask for the advertised price and they'll tell you it went at nine, before their offices even opened. You'll ask how come and they'll tell you they got phone bets, knocking the advertised price down. Rubbish.

In my opinion the big bookmakers also blow back to the race course "phantom" money. If they get a local bet of £1,000, there is nothing to stop them from turning it into a "phantom" £10,000, shortening the price as far as they can and still pull money from the punters. To this very day, out of racing as I am, I cannot put more than a fiver on a horse with any big bookmaker without the price being absolutely slaughtered.

The betting problem got so bad in my last year, 1976, that I was forced to resort to the ultimate weapon: a scrambler on my home telephone. I do not exaggerate. A good friend, ex-Army Intelligence Corps, fitted it for me. He told me, "The code is unbreakable. The frequency changes every twenty seconds on a permutation of an eight-lock timer." What that jargon meant I had no idea, except that anyone listening to my conversation would get nothing but a high frequency tangle of static and gibberish.

Security was my biggest problem as the 1976 season opened, not winners. I had the horses to land the coups, but I had to employ the skills of a counter-spy to thwart the bookmakers, the sporting press, the public, my staff and even my jockeys. If this sounds like paranoia I can assure you that there needed only a pound to appear for a Payne horse and the rush was on to get the bets down before the odds fell through the floor. Even in that last season, before my life came apart at the seams, I saddled thirty-nine winners, and the flat season was not yet concluded.

In my annual battle with the bookies I had a terrifyingly short campaign season. Either I beat them between April and the end of July or I was out of business. The opening month of the flat season was largely unpredictable and by August the hard grounds and the smaller fields of horses made sure-fire gambles that much more difficult. In something like four months. I had to take at least £150,000 away from the bookies in order to maintain my Middleham establishment and keep me in the life-style to which I'd become lovingly accustomed.

Looking back, I don't know how I kept a cool head and a steady hand. But I did. I guess I was hard enough for it. I was born with no money and from my window-cleaning days onward I've accepted that it's all hard graft and wheeling and dealing if you want to make it.

Each night when the battle was on I'd retire to my bedroom early with the form book and the lists of runners for the following day. Not only did I have coups to plan, but I also had the troops to rally: a network of people to phone (hence the scrambler), owners to be told to get in on the betting, other owners to be told their horses would not win the next day. I had to organise my little army of helpers all over the country who would assist in the scattering of my bets around the corner shops. And finally I had to call some of the smaller bookies who would want my advice on what money to keep and what to lay off when the betting came hot and heavy the next day.

These smaller bookies I did not include among my enemies. We duelled and jousted through the racing season, but many of these gentlemen would accept my money out of a sense of honour in their profession, when the big boys would run and hide from me on sight. Many of them helped siphon my money through the system. I tried to see to it that no single small bookie ever got hurt badly by me and, in return, they did me many a favour.

The planning of a big coup might take months, during which a horse was being run in the wrong races, kept less than fit, and used as a red herring for the bookies. The final stage would begin perhaps a week before the day of the gamble itself. First I had to be absolutely sure that the animal was fit and ready and toned up by the vitamins and steroids system. Then at the four-day stage, at which a trainer has to declare all horses previously entered in any races, I'd declare three, four, five—even eight runners in one race.

This always confused the hell out of the racing profession and the sporting press—much to my delight—especially when I left the animals in overnight before the actual race. Indeed a national newspaper once devoted an entire feature article to the £500 in fines I was due to pay on one occasion for late withdrawal of my horses. But it was part of my calculations, an essential element in the planning of a coup. First, I knew that a large field of horses might well be divided into two or three divisions, and splitting the field thus could give my chosen horse a better chance, depending on the split, of course. Second, there were times when I had two horses ready on the same day for a coup in the same race. If the actual starters came up weak, I'd withdraw the better of my two horses, go for the win with the other one and save the better for a coup a couple of days later. This helped confuse the bookies and the punters, because though they might suspect a coup in the offing, they couldn't figure out which horse I was going with. This helped with the odds.

A third factor in my declaring so many horses was the draw. I am a draw fanatic. On some courses it isn't vital, but on others it may mean everything. Every day after the eleven o'clock declarations I would ring up the Press Association, or, in later years, tear off the teleprinter and check the runners and their post positions. If one of my fancied horses had a bad draw I would almost invariably ring up Weatherby's and offer them the well-worn phrase, "Trainer states horse will not run."

It staggers me that this most significant piece of information is still not available to the public in most newspapers on the day of racing. Yet at Catterick, for example, a horse drawn in the middle of the track in a sprint might as well turn around and walk back to the paddock. On most tracks a horse drawn near the running rail has an advantage of up to five lengths. This seems to apply regardless of the ground and even on the straightest of tracks. The Lincoln draw is notorious, but it applies equally on tracks that are otherwise fair.

I was forcibly and expensively reminded of the importance of the draw at Sandown in 1976. It was the Variety meeting, and there were plenty of stars in Sandown's palatial new stands to witness my discomfi-

C. G

ture. I had two horses in the seller, Gaelic God, a sharp horse owned by Peter White, and Imari, owned by Richard Marchant. I spent the day before the race with Richard at his home in Hampstead and passed the evening there studying the field and the draw. Gaelic God had a better draw than Imari and in any case was five lengths better, so I knew where my money was going next day.

I left Imari in, figuring another loss would improve the odds on her and give her a low handicap for the following season. I had plans for her in 1977. Instead, the filly did her little bit—albeit unwittingly, of course—to ensure there'd be no 1977 for me. For I think Gaelic God's owner got the idea that subsequent events were planned by me—and he came in on the "kill" just a few weeks later.

We got to Sandown still happily confident that Gaelic God would trot up. I backed Imari in the ring in my usual fashion just to confuse the bookies, and made my way up to the stand. I moved in next to Les Hall, the Winchester trainer, and said to him, "Where do they start for this race?" Sandown is a confusing track, shaped like a London Transport sign.

"You've been here often enough," said Les. "See for yourself. They're starting right down here on this side."

Appalled, I looked down. My God, what a disaster! The stewards, as they are entitled to do, had shifted the stalls right across the track from their usual side, thus completely reversing the effect of the draw.

Down below I could see the bookies still imperturbably calling Gaelic God as favourite and even letting Imari's price drift. I said to Peter White's brother, John, standing at my side, "They've changed the stalls! They've changed the stalls!" He looked at me blankly, not comprehending yet that we were done for. It was too late to switch out to Imari. There was nothing I could do but watch helplessly as Imari cruised home an easy winner.

As I led Imari in to the usual Variety high jinks, photographs with Dora Bryan and congratulations all around, I had plenty of time to reflect that the reason I was clutching the wrong horse in the Sandown winner's enclosure was that a good draw is worth pounds in weight to any horse. The full implications of Gaelic God's loss were not known to me then. I was to get the really bad news later, when bad news began to come in bunches.

However, there were those happy times when my strategems worked so well I hardly had to get up out of bed to make money. I had spotted a horse I liked which was part of a northern trainer's string. The colt was out of a mare called Lintola which Jack Doyle had once used for a big coup. I remembered him telling me that she was a good, game sort, and to keep an eye on any offspring. This colt of hers had finished fourth in his first outing and I felt that next time out he could be a formidable proposition.

When he was next entered I declared eight of my horses at the four-day stage. I knew this cavalry charge would frighten off all the clever trainers, the Mick Easterbys of this world who might have been planning a little thing of their own. But I hoped it wouldn't frighten off my friend with the Lintola colt. Then at the overnight declaration stage I withdrew all of my eight entries. When I saw which runners were left to challenge my fancied colt I knew my ploy had worked. I put £200 on the colt at 20–1 and didn't even bother going to the races. That was the way I manipulated races up north.

In fact legerdemain and cloak and dagger were necessary weapons when more conventional strategies failed me. I was fighting the bookies' own espionage system all the while. With their network of spies and snoops they can tell you within moments who has been betting on your horse, if he's a regular gambler, or give you a detailed description of the unknown blonde who walked into the corner betting shop and plunked fifty pounds down on a long-priced runner. If she does it again down the street there are enough alarm bells rung around the country to herald an air raid.

The only way to beat them at the spy game was to practice subterfuge and keep my mouth shut. And use a scrambler telephone. Even then my cover was sometimes blown, because the big bookmakers were watching me and my stables like a flock of hawks. Had they devoted half as much energy to external espionage, they'd have all the world's secrets by now. Sometimes my efforts to thwart them became so tangled I'd forget for a few moments myself which horse was the one to back.

There was a splendid comic opera at York in the middle of 1976 when I landed the money to get out of the financial hole for a month or two. The actresses in my little sketch were a pair of fillies named Bowsquare Lady and Bee Bumble. On form, Bee Bumble was much the better filly, having won a non-seller and chalked up a second and a third in good company. But it was Bowsquare Lady, entered in the same five-furlong race, which was the coup horse.

We had given Bowsquare Lady the standard preparations, medicinal and athletic, for the surprise win. We'd run her in a six-furlong seller at Haydock, which was over her distance; she was also in season, and running against horses she couldn't beat. In fact that race was won by Lady Mere. But at five furlongs Bowsquare Lady had been in front, which was all I'd wanted to see. With this prologue satisfactorily completed I went to York and nominated my coup jockey. Tommy Lappin, to ride Bee Bumble. I then reinforced the impression that she was the form horse by going around taking every price I could get on her until I had a thousand pounds going on a horse I knew wouldn't win.

Meanwhile, down in the south of England I had a

team of old friends from the New Forest making the rounds of the betting shops from Maidenhead to the West End backing Bowsquare Lady. This was the kind of coup that called for such organisation, and even then I faced the risk that somebody would be tempted to put too much on the horse and give the game away.

But this time the game worked to perfection. As Eccles, my apprentice jockey, took Bowsquare Lady, and Lappin cantered Bee Bumble down to the York start, there was total confusion in the ring. Everyone knew there was money flying around for one of Payne's horses, everyone knew I was up to one of my old dodges, but nobody knew with which horse. I treasure to this day a videotape of the race by ITV in which the commentator, poor John Oaksey, was trying to sort them out. One minute he was telling everyone Bee Bumble was the favourite, the next he'd say it was Bowsquare Lady. Then back to Bee Bumble.

It was no better during the running of the race; the poor chap couldn't tell one from the other. Watching wryly through the glass from the fourth floor of the York stands I thought that Major Sanderson's turf owed me something for the number of times luck had gone against me by a neck or a short head. This time I was certain there'd be no mistakes, and indeed Bowsquare Lady romped home in a canter with six or seven lengths to spare.

I walked straight to the lift, descended to the car park, liberated my Jag and drove to London for the rendezvous with my team. The odds had been 4–1 and 7–2 and the pile of bookies' money had never looked so good to me. I made the payout, and walked off with a paper bag stuffed with over £20,000. But that amount of money is heavy, and so I went into a greengrocer's in Marylebone High Street and asked to buy a plastic carrier bag. He was just closing, and he put on his high-class fruiterer's voice and said to me, "I'm sorry, I sell fruit, not carrier bags."

I said, "Okay then, I'll have a tenner's worth of fruit and a carrier bag."

Solemnly he weighed out a Christmas hamper's worth of apples, pears and oranges and handed the lot to me. I'll never forget the look on his face when I dumped them all out again on his counter and began transferring notes from the paper bag to the plastic one. He must have thought I'd just robbed a bank. When I'd finished the transfer I took one of the apples, bit into it, gave him a broad wink, and went on my way.

Another memorable episode began during a bit of off-track mayhem. I was watching a Stanley Baker film on TV one Sunday afternoon and it got to the bit where it looked as though Stanley's craggy good looks were about to be altered, when the phone rang. A voice said, "I want to buy a selling plater. I've been in racing for seven years and all I want is a winner."

I said to the guy, "Look, nobody buys selling platers. You just kind of get landed with them. But you sound like my sort of guy. Ring me back in twenty minutes when the film is over and we'll talk about it."

Twenty minutes later he rang back. His name was Michael Taylor, he was an estate agent from Lancashire, and he insisted on buying a horse. Over the phone I sold him a filly I'd recently bought for myself called Mistress X. "She's running at Haydock in a couple of weeks," I told Michael. "But don't go putting money on her. I'm planning to let her win at Carlisle next time out after that."

Fillies are temperamental creatures, however, and Mistress X began to give us a bad time. She refused to gallop, kicked up her heels and dug in her toes like a real headstrong young lady. But Tommy Lappin brought her home fourth at Haydock and as he unsaddled he said to me, "I know how to ride her. She'll win next time."

She continued to raise a ruckus each morning when she went out with the string, but still I was confident. Every time Lappin galloped her she showed good speed and I began laying plans for a big gamble at Carlisle.

Then, the day before the race, with a lot of planning already gone into the gamble, Lappin fell off and broke his collar bone. But I figured John Curant could handle her and I took him up to Carlisle with me. Michael Taylor and his lovely wife were standing proudly in the paddock admiring their filly when the call came over the tannoy, "Jockeys, please mount." I gave Curant a leg up; instantly there was a flurry and he landed at Mrs. Taylor's feet. We tried again. Again Curant landed on the floor. We tried a third time, got horse and rider at last on to the track, where she unseated him again.

This time she didn't wait around. The filly took off across the track, overtook the other cantering runners, did a return trip past the winning post and then took a fancy to the National Hunt track that runs inside the flat circuit at Carlisle. To roars of approval from the crowd she leaped three of the jumps including the water, then stopped, good as gold, to be caught. I laughed myself, shrugging off a mislaid coup. At least the stake money would be safe. I turned away to climb the stands, figuring of course that they'd bring the filly in and she'd not go under starter's orders. Not after that wild gallop. Michael grinned at me. "Maybe we should put her in the National," he said.

"Maybe you're right," I said. Then, looking down to the start, I almost fell out of the stands. I couldn't believe it. John Curant was being given a lift to the gate and Mistress X, instead of being led away to be unsaddled, was being brought down for him to ride.

"My God!" I cried out, "they're going to run her!" I leaped out of the stands and ran down towards the track. There was an old chap sitting in a Land Rover nearby, one of the course staff, and I rushed up to him. "I'll give you twenty quid to drive me down to the start!"

"But they're about to start the race!"

"That's the point," I said. "With us in the middle of the track they can't."

The rest was Keystone Kops. With shouts from the police and track officials pursuing us, the Land Rover careered down the middle of the course to the starting gate. The starter was waving his white flag and jumping up and down. Curant was sitting in the saddle, a silly grin on his face. "She's all right," he said to me.

"The hell she is," I replied. "She'll never win and you, John, are suddenly feeling very ill indeed from your fall."

"I guess I am at that," he said, with a sigh of relief. He dismounted, we took Mistress X away from there, and with immense relief I saw the starter reassemble the herd and send them off. I'd deprived the bookies of a birthday by a whisker.

On the way back to the stands I met one of the local vets. "I was going to claim that filly of yours," he said to me. "Shame she didn't run."

At that moment I'd have taken a hundred quid for her as dog meat. But I said to him, "Well, she'll be running again."

"She could have been claimed for £1,200, couldn't she?" the vet persisted. "I'll give you that for her."

"Look," I said, "bring a cheque up to me in the stands made out to Michael Taylor for £1,100 and you can have her, bridle and all."

When I got to the unsaddling enclosure Michael was all in a lather. "How is she?" he asked.

"How's who?"

"My horse."

"You don't have a horse any more," I told him. "I just sold her." He didn't know whether to laugh or cry, but I said to him, "Just take the money and be thankful. We can't afford to mess around with a creature like that."

The vet duly arrived with the cheque, and Michael and I figured we'd come out of it with a good day's racing, all things considered. And I was glad enough to see that some time later the vet even won a race with the filly.

In my last year of racing, when my machinations became ever more intricate, I sometimes was able to make a plunge through some of the few extraordinary individualists still around in the betting game. These are the Stallion brothers, for whom I trained, Micky Tabor and, tucked away in his offices near Piccadilly, Chummy Gaventa. None of them could entirely stop my bets from getting back to the track and killing the price, but they would have a damned good try.

Chummy is one of the last of the old-time characters, a commission agent who takes his cut from other bookmakers out of the business he brings them. His offices are like the plushest of private clubs. None of the clutter and clatter of a betting shop, none of the indignity of betting slips. Tea and refreshments are served to the clientele while they murmur their requirements to members of Chummy's staff. The man himself stands with his back to the wall with a battery of telephones in front of him, taking and transmitting wagers. It is all very underplayed, but the name of Chummy's game is timing. Everyone is trying to hold off betting until the last handler is ducking out from under the starting stalls. The idea is to prevent a price change, despite a sudden heavy load of cash on a horse. A very tricky business, and Chummy's an expert at it.

He selected me as a trainer by the simple command, "Payne, I've heard about you. I pay my bills and a few quid over. I'm sending you three horses." But when my activities started to hit some of his business colleagues, he took them away again just as abruptly, with another phone call. "Payne, you're too hot for me. I'm taking my horses away." But he'd always take a bet from me, even though it went down on the course pretty quickly afterward.

Right up to the end I had a couple of bookies who would be willing to do me favours, especially in return for a bit of useful information. One day, for example, I was at Lanark, confident that I was saddling the winners of the first two races. But the prices were derisory. I also had a runner going in the first race at Catterick which would be a loser, although it was a hot overnight favourite with the bookmakers. This was Rhonda Prince, the horse I had originally bought for Stanley Baker. I knew he'd lose because I'd placed him there to lose. The distance was too short. I reckoned Pal Dan the winner, a horse trained by my Middleham neighbour, Harry Blackshaw.

I went up to a bookmaker who had found it rewarding to take my advice in the past and asked him if he had a lot of money for Rhonda Prince; he had a small string of betting shops in the north. He told me that he was holding quite a bit, and that he was planning to lay most of it off.

"Keep it all," I said. "Pal Dan will beat him."

He looked surprised. "Are you sure?"

I nodded. He thanked me and went away to make a few phone calls.

Catterick was off before Lanark, and Pal Dan duly obliged us. The bookie had made a lot of money and he gave me a "Thank You" of £500. That was chicken feed compared with the £10,000 he then helped me lift off his colleagues on the course by providing me with the help only one of his fraternity could provide. On the first race my horse opened at 2–1 and soon shortened to evens. But my friend began to shout loudly at 3–1 and the punters gathered around him like wasps on a jam pot. The big bookies had to follow him or lose the business. When they joined him at 3–1 he went to 4–1 and then 5–1

At the last moment, naturally, through his regular on-course helpers, he laid off all the money at the starting price.

We repeated the game for the second race. By then everyone knew the score, but there was little that could be done about it. The big bookmakers had to stay with him or lose all the business. Even if they only went to 3–1 when he was proclaiming 5–1, the ring inspector was bound to report a starting price of at least 4–1.

It was a lovely day, but both the bookie and I knew that such shenanigans could not be repeated often.

I loved the fun and games, but the strain was beginning to tell on me. Down through the years I'd suffered the occasional recurrence of a malaria attack; now they were becoming more frequent and more severe. I was pushing myself too hard, wheeling and dealing and driving myself—even playing too hard. I was run down, my resistance lowered, vulnerable to the little bug that still lived on in my bloodstream.

Neither was it all just fun and games. I would not like to pretend that there wasn't a heavier side to my racing, when the big money was down and people stood to win or lose, collect or pay out six figure sums. I got a whiff of the grape shot one day in 1976 up at Hamilton, in Scotland.

Ironically, I thought I was in for some easy money, without even having to organise it for myself. I even stopped Jack Doyle from going home to Ireland with the promise that we could go up to Hamilton, collect, and he could then be on his way to Glasgow airport within an hour or two.

I had spotted something fishy about a horse running up there called Katmandu. He was owned by John Banks the bookmaker and trained by Frank Carr, a man who'd spiked one or two plots of mine in the past. I was pleased enough, therefore, at the chance to make some money out of him, particularly as I could always get bets down at the racecourse when I was backing an animal with which I had no connections.

Katmandu had been placed cleverly. He was well bred and hadn't had a hard race in good company all year. Even so, his connections had picked out a race in which I had a runner that would be fancied. Thus I would be making the odds for them. My horse, Oswaldton, would be the overnight favourite and might well stay that way till off time, despite heavy betting off the track on Katmandu. I of all people knew that if smart money was planning a caper with Katmandu the betting would be well scattered and well disguised.

That was fine with me. Katmandu certainly figured to beat my horse by my calculations, so I saw no reason why I shouldn't cut myself in as a silent partner in the coup. But the bookmakers who were hatching it, and no doubt planning to leave their bigger brothers, like Hills and Ladbroke's, holding a very large and squalling baby, began to get cold feet. Something began to worry them, as I soon found out.

It was an evening meeting at Hamilton and I was already on the late side for the sprint up to Glasgow when the phone rang. I heard the pips go, indicating a coin-box call. I answered, and an unfamiliar voice said, "Are you Payne?"

"That's right."

"I'm interested in buying a number of race-horses and I understand you may have some in your yard for sale. Can you tell me about them?"

"Sure. But I'm in a bit of a hurry right now. Are you calling me from your office? Give me the number and I'll call you back tomorrow."

"Yeah, I'm at my office." The thought came to me that it was a funny office with only a coin-box phone. Then he said to me, "You got a horse running tonight called Oswaldton. Will he win?"

"I don't know. He might do. Listen, I'm sorry but I've got to go." I hung up, annoyed at yet another lunatic caller looking for a tip on a horse.

A minute later the phone rang again. Exasperated, I picked it up. Although there was an overly theatrical attempt to disguise the voice I knew it was the same caller. This time he was more to the point.

"Oswaldton better not win tonight if you ever want to drive a car again."

The phone went click.

I didn't like it. I didn't like it at all. I'd had threats before, including one ominously detailing the time and place at which my son Seth left school and warning of all sorts of horrors to be perpetrated. I'd reported that one to the police, and nothing had ever come of it, fortunately. But somehow there was an edge to this one which, combined with the circumstances of the race, had a special menace to it. I was certain that neither the owner nor the trainer had anything to do with it. I'd always enjoyed the best of relations with John Banks. He was the kind of bookie who'd take a big bet from you, pay you out with a smile and even buy you a drink. I had the utmost respect and regard for him.

Still, I put the threat aside and went up to Hamilton. When I got to the track, the first person I met was Harry Beeby, the Doncaster bloodstock auctioneer. Harry also conducted the bidding after the sellers on many of the northern racecourses.

"What have you heard from London, Ken?" he said. "There are all sorts of rumours floating about."

"I haven't talked to London yet," I said, and went away to the phone.

I soon got the word from my friends in London that there was some very big money indeed flying about. Even one of my owners was in on it, standing to win some £30,000. I told my own connections that I thought

Katmandu would win and that I was backing him with my own money. Then I got the truly big news: there was a gamble going in the first race as well, with Katmandu in the second race bringing in the second half of a colossal double.

As I walked away from the phone boxes the first person I saw was Katmandu's owner, John Banks. A lot of eyes were on us as we met, and afterwards I heard that people thought he'd asked me to stop Oswaldton. It never happened. All he said to me was, "What do you think will win, Kenny?"

"Katmandu," I told him.

He laughed. "Not shown much form so far."

I walked into the Hamilton enclosure. The atmosphere was electric, crackling with stories about the impending coup. And for the first time I sensed that the big gamble might well go down the drain. Because the planners had overlooked three items, any one of which could ruin them.

First, their greed. A double coup was stretching your luck. Too many things can go wrong during the running of a race to chance two consecutive races going exactly right. Second, the ground was against Katmandu. Third, they had paid insufficient attention to the jockeys for the crucial second leg. In his previous four or five races, Oswaldton had been ridden by one of my apprentices, because his owner, Douglas Lowry, had taken a dislike to Tommy Lappin. But now after a string of poor runs by his horse, Mr. Lowry had asked me to put Lappin back on. On Hamilton's punishing uphill run-in I knew Lappin would be a tough customer against any rider in Britain. In a tight finish Chris Dwyer, Katmandu's jockey, would be no match for Tommy.

I wondered after all if I ought to put a saver on my horse and advise my friends to do the same. I shelved the thought for the moment, as the horses cantered to the post for the first race and the first leg of the big coup.

I must tell it as I saw it: it was the most disgraceful race I have ever seen on a British track. The horse that was the public favourite was blatantly slow out of the start. Had I been sitting him, facing his tail, I could have got him away quicker than that. A couple of other horses were no faster, and by the time all the dilatory riders finally got their horses' legs untangled the first half of the big gamble was home and dry. It was the most outrageous piece of manipulation I have ever witnessed. Indeed I was staggered that anyone would even try it on a British track. The crowd was muttering in disbelief and stood there buzzing until the outcome of the inevitable enquiry was announced. It took the stewards almost till the start of the second race to announce that the result would stand. Whatever their suspicions, there was no way to prove anything.

Clearly I had to go and make another phone call to London. "It still looks like Katmandu," I said. "But the ground's not in his favour and if it's close at all I don't fancy Dwyer's chances if he's got Lappin up his backside in a finish."

"Well," my contact said, "there's an awful lot of your friend's money here that says you're wrong."

In all honesty I don't know what I would have done in ordinary circumstances; perhaps tell Tommy not to give Oswaldton too hard a ride. But after the farce of that first race, anyone who did not give his jockey instructions to get out there and ride like hell to win risked being warned off from racing for life—especially if he was a known gambling trainer. No, there was no way I could give Tommy Lappin any order other than to win—threats, gambles and friendships notwithstanding.

By the time the jockeys were let out to canter down for the start of the second race, everyone at the track must have guessed what was coming off. You could feel it in the air. There was a strange hush over the course, a subdued murmuring. A flood of money from London had suddenly deluged the track and I think the whole of Scotland knew where it was going. There was no way of knowing how much was riding on Katmandu that night, but later I was told that the £30,000 my friend was shooting for was not the largest bet down, not by a long shot.

The start was as clean as a whistle and as they hit the rise Lappin had Oswaldton tucked in tight behind Katmandu. A furlong out he was still there, and I watched with hypnotised fascination. With half a furlong to go Lappin pulled out with Oswaldton and moved him up alongside Dwyer on Katmandu. I noted again, at that precise moment, the eerie silence on the course. There was not the usual cheering and shouting as the two horses fought out the final few hundred yards. Neck and neck they were, the jockeys slashing with their whips—and then the silence was shattered by an explosion of shouting as Lappin got Oswaldton's nose out in front and hit the wire to win by a head.

John Banks walked over to me and said, with a grin, "Your horse ran the race of his life tonight, Kenny."

"No, he just had a different jockey," I said.

I never heard anything more of the threat, or of the huge sums that were "done" by a lot of people I knew. But the next day just one sentence from a friend in London told me all. He said to me, shaking his head sadly, "Oh Kenny. What did you do last night?"

CHAPTER FOURTEEN

THE Heathrow to Teeside route is not the most glamorous flight out of London airport. But that Thursday the crew of the British Midlands turbo-prop Viscount were being as fussily exact as though it were the maiden flight of Concorde. The doors were closed, the No Smoking and Fasten Your Seat Belt signs were on. The hostess double-checked the passenger manifest. Then she intoned the "Welcome aboard this British Midlands Airways flight" routine.

I'd heard it all before. I'd used the flight like a bus run ever since I'd moved my yard to Middleham. But that Thursday afternoon, that cold, grim Thursday afternoon in October of 1976, I knew that familiar flight was taking me back to what was certainly the end of my career as a racing trainer. Despite the cold, despite the chill in the aircraft, my shirt was wringing wet, soaked through to my skin. Malaria was hitting me again and my mind, whirling with fever and a thousand problems, turned on my sweat glands like a million leaky bath taps.

As the plane began to glide from its pod, the stewardess approached me. "Would you mind putting that bag under your seat, Mr. Payne? The rack is only for coats and hats."

As a matter of fact, anyone on the plane would have been happy enough to have that supermarket carrier bag fall on his head. It contained just over twelve thousand pounds in used notes of every denomination that the bookmaker had been able to rustle up in a hurry. I had been too lethargic to bother transferring the money into my leather grip. I guess I had a thing for carting money around in carrier bags, a defiant gesture of I-couldn't-care-less.

But the stewardess' words irritated me for some reason. My mind was on a hair-trigger anyway. I stood up abruptly and said to her, "I'm feeling ill. I'll have to get off this plane." She didn't argue, but went straight back up the flight deck. I probably looked ill. In any case the crew all knew me. If I wanted to get off the plane, then that's what I ought to do. It rocked to a halt. A minute later the steps appeared and I was ushered off the plane. Stupidly, dazedly, I put the carrier bag down on the tarmac and watched the plane taxi away. A gust of wind swept across the parking bay. The carrier bag toppled over. I grabbed at it, but a few notes spilled out. I just stood there and looked at them as the wind carried them across the tarmac, heading for Slough. A few less, a few more, what did it all mean?

Back in the departure lounge at Terminal One I sat and contemplated the obvious. I owed the banks in excess of £100,000; the overdraft at Lloyds Bank Catterick alone was eighty grand, and I had lesser accounts at other banks here and there—all in the red. That in itself was not unusual. And the banks were being more than kind. So long as I had a few solid winners in the boxes and a good string of yearlings to bring on in the new year, there'd always be a gamble or two in the offing to keep the banks happy. The trouble was, it looked as though there soon wouldn't be any horses.

The temptation was to take the twelve thousand and stash it somewhere safe for the day when the rest of my world collapsed around me—which looked as though it might be as soon as tomorrow. Ten years in racing had taught me enough to know the places to put pound notes if you wanted to. The trouble was, that was not my style.

I'd always played it straight in my business relationships, paid my dues when the bills came; paid them late more often than not, but paid them all the same. And I wasn't going down now with a bagful of other people's money. The fact that I even contemplated such a move indicated my state of mind.

For months I had been living a caricature of myself: Ken Payne, high-living, buccaneering race-horse trainer. That's how the newspapers regularly portrayed me. Well, at that moment I didn't feel very much like a buccaneer, more like a man preparing to walk the plank. I sat there in the terminal, gloomily trying to sort out my thoughts, despairing of coming to any useful decision, hoping that as I sat there some miracle would occur and make a decision for me. Like a bomb falling on my head.

But by the time the last flight was called for Teesside airport on that black Thursday in October, I knew, as I suppose I had really known all along, that I had to go back to Middleham and face the music. The carrier bag would go to Lloyds Bank.

The year had been a bad one for a lot of trainers. For me, catastrophic. My stables, my estranged wife and my girl friends were costing me close on a quarter of a million pounds a year to run. Every week I needed £4,000 just to pay the wages and the bills. The only people who could provide that sort of money were the bookmakers. And for eight years they had.

But the freakish hot weather and the concrete-hard grounds of 1976 had put a cramp in my system. Horses could not run, meetings were cancelled, form was upset, the carefully planned gambles that were my lifeblood were impossible in the eccentric and erratic conditions. Inflation, too, was bludgeoning me and my owners. Feed bills were rocketing. Hay had gone to £2 a bale and forty lads and staff had to be paid and fed.

And yet these financial problems were not the principal

cause of my distress. I could handle banks and bookmakers. I had learned to wheel and deal with the best of them ever since that day—Lord, how many years ago was it?—when I bought myself a bucket and ladder with borrowed money and set myself up as Ken Payne Window Cleaning. Digging myself out of financial holes had been my life for so long I knew no other way.

No, I could have handled all of that. But 1976 had been a tough year for me in other ways; tough where I didn't know how to fight. In March, just as the flat season was getting under way, my youngest son, Nathan, had been killed when a bale of straw fell on him at his grandfather's farm. Lynda and I had separated and she'd taken the boys with her to stay at her parents' farm in the New Forest.

It had not been an easy separation. We battled constantly from afar. Even after Nathan died I found myself in court, week after week, fighting for access to my other two sons, Seth and Joss. Usually to no avail. Somehow, through legal manoeuvres or otherwise, she managed to keep me apart from them. My distress was unbearable. I couldn't work and I couldn't rest. All of this brought the malaria back again. I lost weight, became a walking skeleton.

But it was Nathan that haunted me the most.

When I got back to Middleham and Kingsley House that Thursday night I went straight to bed. But sleep would not give me its blessing. I lay there, staring at the ceiling, remembering. Kingsley House was a big rambling house set back behind magnificent trees beside the church in Middleham. In the happy days of 1972 when I'd arrived and surrounded it with brand-new boxes and a hundred horses it had seemed the archetypal happy family house with my wife and children hurtling about and visitors or owners staying with us.

Now—vast, overbearing, empty in the damp darkness of the October night, it seemed like one of the more banal settings for a Hammer film. Certainly it had ghosts for me. I got up out of bed and wandered into Nathan's room. I found it impossible to comprehend that he was dead.

I was still in that pathetic mood the next morning; maudlin, overflowing with self-pity, if you will. Yes, I felt sorry for myself; sorry for my boy, sorry for a lot of things. I was crying when Ken Mitchard came to fetch me. My head lad, who had been with me almost from the start and who had taken virtually sole charge of the horses, tried to cheer me up.

"Come up and see the yearlings work, boss. They're a cracking lot."

He drove me up to Middleham Moor. As usual there were hundreds of horses from the sixteen Middleham stables working out on the moor, cantering and galloping, trying out the stalls, trotting on the roads. What a sight to swell a horseman's heart on a misty October morning! And how it hurt, knowing I might never see such a sight again, never again be a part of such a scene. There, amongst them, was my own string, the largest string of them all, cantering down the steep slope at the middle of the gallops towards Sam Hall's beautiful place at Spigot Lodge, with the breathtaking and vertiginous view down the dale towards the ruins of Castle Bolton.

It was cold and wet but already many of the yearlings were broken and backed and knew enough about their work to do a little two-furlong gallop. There was no doubt that the crop of thirty yearlings Jack Doyle had brought me that September was probably the best bunch we had ever had. Whether we would manage to pay for them was another matter.

Ken Mitchard came up to me. For a moment he just stood there. Then he said, "You're never going to see him again, guv', hanging over the back of that Land Rover and you tellin' him to get back in to avoid the bumps.

Nathan's dead. And I'll tell you this. If you want to get out of this game, think about yourself. Don't think about us. You've been a good boss to us. We'll be all right."

I turned and walked off the Middleham gallops for the last time and drove straight to Teesside airport. On the plane back to London I kept thinking: if only I could get my head together, surely I could figure a way out of all this. I was so numb, so befuddled, punchy. My brain felt soft as a sponge. I'd try to concentrate on business but after a few seconds, no more, my mind would stray again to Nathan, to those irritating, infuriating phone calls from Lynda, and I'd sink once again into abysmal despair.

In London I went to meet Jack Doyle and two of my owners, Richard Marchant and John Fitzpatrick, in Richard's flat in Park Lane. We had dinner but it was more like a wake than a party. We talked about my money troubles and my family problems and the prospects for the coming year. Even in 1976, I had pulled off some tremendous gambles for Richard and John; new to racing, Richard had had five winners, a quite remarkable start.

Jack Doyle urged me to go back and set myself straight. "You're the leading trainer in the North. Get Lynda and the banks sorted out and we can have a marvellous year next year. You know you've got the horses to do it."

On the Sunday afternoon I drove down to see Lynda in Hampshire. She was bitter and scathing and unwilling even to discuss the financial settlement I offered her. On Monday afternoon I went back to Middleham.

As I walked through the door the phone was ringing. It was the bank. I put them off until the following day; they'd had the £12,000. There was a pile of mail. I didn't care to look, but my secretary, Angela, said there were some personal letters waiting for me in my study. I went in and shuffled through them. Opened the first one. It was from one of my owners, Peter White (Gaelic God, among others). I hadn't seen much of Peter since the Royal Ascot meeting that year. I had taken him with me to lunch with one of the kindest and most thoughtful of my owners, Sir Norman Hartnell. Sir Norman, the Royal dressmaker, had entertained us in regal style at his house near Ascot and we had then gone on for the afternoon's racing. In the evening Peter, his brother John, and their wives had accompanied me on the town. Unhappily that evening had ended disastrously, with an affray at dinner.

I began reading the letter with a sinking feeling, a justifiable prescience on my part. It announced that he had entered my yard, without my permission, decided the animals weren't being kept properly, and that he was withdrawing his horses. It went on to say that obviously I was not well enough to train, and that his action would relieve some of the pressure on me. I was stung; but the implication about the treatment of his horses was really a twist of the knife. Apparently he had come on the Sunday, the one day my lads were off, and when the boxes were not all necessarily cleaned out. I suppose he hadn't stopped to consider that.

The next letter was even more wounding. Richard Marchart, in whose flat I had had dinner that very weekend and whom I had introduced so successfully to racing, wrote saying he too didn't feel I was well enough to continue training. He was moving his horses immediately.

As I lay on the bed, unable to sleep, unable to think straight, the phone rang. It was John Fitzpatrick, the third member of the week-end party. His message was the same.

Obviously it was the end.

I got up and wandered about the house, down to the office, into the study, along to the great front room that looked across to Captain Neville Crump's house. Neville is a great trainer, and for all his shouting he had been a good friend and a help to me in Middleham. But his world of titled owners and great horses was a long way from mine of selling platers and desperate gambles. Once, eons ago, I had had the temerity to entertain thoughts of joining him. That was all over now.

I climbed back up the stairs. Went into Nathan's room. He was there, in his bed. I remembered how many times he would come into my room, walking in his sleep, and crawl into my bed to sleep the night with me. Nathan. He would have been four years old in another week or so, had he lived.

I saw him there still, awake now, smiling at me, calling to me, reaching out to me . . . and I thought, yes, I'll join my boy, I'll go to him, and to hell with everything else.

I went back to my room and swallowed a bottle of pills.

Then I began to write some letters. Bizarrely I picked out some "Peanuts" notepaper instead of the Kingsley House pad and, under a cartoon of Charlie Bubbles saying, "Someone's been playing Fetch with my pencil," I wrote ten letters of farewell.

To Ken Mitchard I wrote:

"Please forgive me but I can't take anymore. It seems that I am a nuisance and an embarrassment now. John Fitzpatrick has just phoned about his horses. I can't bear to see it all broken up. Thanks for everything. You have been my best friend. God bless. Please forgive me, perhaps we'll meet again one day. Get Jack Doyle if you need help. He really is a friend but I can't help myself at the moment. I have no money free to do the things which should be done."

To my bank manager, John Shoppe:

"John, I hope I don't get you into too much trouble. You have been a father to me. But things go wrong and I don't feel strong enough to fight any more. Anyway I can't face the emptiness without my family here."

There were others to my children, to owners who had

been close friends and to my doctor. I sealed them up and swallowed some more pills.

It was ironic that the man who found me stiff and cold on the floor the next morning and who gave me the kiss of life repeatedly until he got a spark of response from my heart, was the same man who had pursued me relentlessly through the courts on an issue involving theft. Of one thing I am certain I have never stolen so much as a button in my whole life. From the first moment I got on a race course I knew you didn't have to steal. Betting was easier. And it was legal.

I have never been back to Middleham since the night I tried to commit suicide. But there have been planty of people to tell me what happened in the wake of that dreadful October evening. Had it not been so tragic, it would have been bordering on the hilarious.

Middleham is a tiny place considering there are sixteen trainers and four hundred or so horses needing looking after. It stands around a little market square underneath a ruined castle. Two narrow roads, one from Coverdale and the other from Upper Wensleydale meet and meander away down towards the Vale of York, the A1, and the dozen or so race courses that had been my battlefields down through the years.

The War of the Roses must have been the last time the little town saw as much activity as on the day the news broke that Ken Payne was on the verge of death and his empire was collapsing. There was near panic in the streets and the vultures came screeching down in case there were pickings to be had.

I am told that the roads in and out of Middleham were jammed with horse boxes as owners scrambled to get their hands on their horseflesh. The police had padlocked the big iron gates of Kingsley House, but not before there had been a fist fight between two owners in the gravel drive over who owned a particular horse. Despite all the claims and counterclaims, there was really no cause for any of that. If only some of the impetuous types had not stampeded at the prospect of my demise.

True, the ownership of some of my horses was split, even syndicated among a number of small owners. Often I kept a piece for myself in order to retain a say in the animal's future, so that I was not entirely at the mercy of an owner's whim or the petulance of his wife or girl friend. Syndicating, which is still popular, is also a way to give the little guy a chance at the thrill of owning a horse and seeing his colours racing. The system broke down on that October day only because owners were trundling their boxes into the yard, asking the first lad they saw which was their horse, taking his word, and loading the animals up. The situation was made worse by the presence of thirty yearlings in the boxes, some of them still not fully syndicated and registered. The only authority on who owned what as of October 25, 1976, was me, and I was in a coma in Northallerton Friarage Hospital.

Eventually the ownership problem sorted itself out. No horse today is running under the wrong colours.

A lot of people in Middleham rallied around me. Sam Hall sent one of his senior lads, John Wade, to offer some hay. Dickie Peacock, another fine horseman who had always been kind to me in Middleham, offered his help. Other trainers chipped in with feed and a willingness to take any horses that were left behind. Their help was needed, because there were plenty of other people who were falling over each other to get what was left of the pickings. A couple of removal vans arrived while I was in hospital and stripped the house clean. There was hardly a light fitting left.

Ken Mitchard and the lads carried on for a few days, looking after what horses were left, often with the help of money from some of my best owners, like Michael Taylor. But there were no wages for them and eventually they left. Many of them took their work saddles and tack in lieu of wages. The cars and the Land Rover went. All the new wooden horse-boxes I'd installed were dismantled and taken away again. Kingsley House must have been a forlorn sight. (Steve Nesbitt bought the place late in 1977, and I wish him the best of luck in the world with it.)

There is no doubt some people suffered, but I hope to repay them one day when all my troubles are sorted out. Richard Marchant and John Fitzpatrick, the two owners whose decision to remove their horses had contributed to my collapse, proved sterling friends afterward; John even stood up to a substantial guarantee for me with Tattersalls.

As I write this, the shock waves of the cataclysm that nearly destroyed me are still receding, leaving me shaking yet, but coming out of it, putting together the broken pieces of my life. I have a flat in London and wonderful girl to share it with me. I paint, transferring to canvas those scenes that are warmest in my memory . . . the New Forest, fresh and green in spring, tawny gold and crimson in autumn . . . yearlings, romping over the gallops . . . jockeys on their mounts, cantering down to the starting gate.

Maybe I'll paint for a living. Who knows?

I know only this. Duke Payne has been battered about and knocked down. But he will be up again, even if, as his old sergeant-major used to say of him, he has to stand up twice to make a shadow.

EPILOGUE

MY WARNINGS about the parlous state of British racing, its sad decline since my days as an apprentice with Atty Persse, don't arise from sour grapes. Even in a small yard such as Atty's, we had horses like Durante and Queen of Sheba and Spartan Sacrifice. Now there are few of that calibre anywhere in Britain.

Anyone who has been to racing in France or the United States knows how far behind we have fallen. It is not only that our best bloodstock is being exported, that even countries like Poland can now outbid us for as smart a horse as Dakota, that animal after animal is knocked down to the Japanese at every sale. Our whole attitude to racing is light years behind the Americans and the Continentals. Yet it is we who are the richest in knowledge, in expertise, in history, even in climate and environment. There are no jockeys in the world to touch the top-flight British riders. The thoroughbred evolved here and, despite some of the dilettantes, I maintain that British trainers can still call upon unrivalled stocks of experience.

In my view drastic remedies are required. I would abolish the Jockey Club and abolish the bookmakers. Both in their ways are parasites on racing. The Jockey Club perpetuates that curious English assumption that if you have an Etonian accent and a country house then you somehow are qualified to dictate to people who are in every other way your superiors. The Jockey Club has further refined this theory by requiring an Army commission (retired) and a special uniform of brown trilby and green jacket before you are admitted to the ranks of those appointed to mete out justice to the toilers on the tracks.

I am hardly a propagator of class warfare, but I believe class is in the man, not in his superficial trappings. Some of the ennobled gentlemen I have met in racing are truly the salt of the earth and each gentlemen in every sense of the word; others I wouldn't give a job as a stable lad, for fear they'd fall down and hurt themselves mucking out a horse-box. It is a matter of amazement to me that the true professionals in racing have done so little to challenge the antediluvian attitude of the Jockey Club. Jockeys, owners and trainers meekly submit to diktats from the most ignorant of stewards and the most autocratic of Jockey Club regimes.

Even the stable lads took years to get themselves in any way organised and they are still a long way from making their presence felt. The fact is that the stable lads are the one group which could close racing down if they united, but they remain disorganised and devoted to their jobs. It is this disunity within the whole professional side of racing that has allowed the Jockey Club to retain its power for so long.

I see no way, or any reason, to reform the Jockey Club. It should be painlessly put down and replaced at every level in the administration of racing by people who have had long experience on the professional side of racing, together with those who have put their time and money into the game as owners.

I would like to see equal root and branch action taken with the bookmakers. Other than window-dressing, I can't think of a single thing they provide to the benefit of either the racing industry or the racing public. A few races sponsored here and there are a drop in the ocean compared with vast fortunes annually and blatantly milked out of the betting shops of Britain into private pockets or public extravagances. The pittance that the Levy Board collects has provided some artificial respiration for racing at a time when it might have died, sucked dry by the vampires in the check suits and big cigars.

All betting should be through the Tote. It is fair, it is not open to manipulation by insiders like myself, and it is not run for anyone's profit except, perhaps, those entitled to take a share—the Government and the racing industry. At a stroke many of our racing ills would be cured. There would be vastly greater prize money which, as in France and in the United States, does nothing but good. It provides better racing for the public, allows owners to support the best horses, reduces chicanery by jockeys and trainers, simply because you can race for the prize money and not the gamble. It also would encourage breeders to stay in the game.

The fact that the Tote has been so badly operated in the last few years does not alter the fact that a Tote monopoly would be the most important single contribution to a revival of British racing and bloodstock breeding.

Even in the short term, and without waiting for the inevitable extinction of the two bodies on my extermination list, there are things that can be done to give racing a much-needed transfusion. For one, the myths of betting must be dispelled. It seems our Members of Parliament imagine that the average punter (whoever that is) carefully works out his day's wagers during his morning tea break, bolts down his sandwiches at lunch in order to get his bets down, and then collects his winnings on his way home from work. All this, without lingering for an extra moment in the betting shop or robbing his employer of a minute of his services. Betting shops, in fact, are deliberately kept as appetizing as a motorway caff to discourage the punter from hanging about, as outrageous a piece of hypocrisy as I have ever come across.

The truth is that hundreds of thousands of men manage to find the time to spend hours in the betting shops every afternoon. Racing should profit from it. Television should be permitted, with a transmission fee to be paid to the race track. Indeed, racing has been singularly slow to take advantage of the precedents set by the Football League and now even by the greyhound men. Revenue gained from transmission fees should be put into prize money and into providing a few decent amenities at the tracks.

The courses themselves are in need of rationalisation and a thorough shake-up. I would certainly not weep to see the demise of places like Sedgefield and Hamilton. Local racegoers could easily be compensated by extra days of racing at other tracks in the area. In America they think nothing of racing a month or more on the same track. Some of the big tracks in the London area and near other big cities could easily support double, and even treble, the number of racing days presently allotted to them. This would have the beneficial effect of establishing a regular clientele, bringing money into the coffers for building better facilities both for horses and for the public, and enabling the tracks to spend money ironing out the worst aberrations of the racing surface itself.

The day must come when comfortable, efficient, all-weather tracks are the norm here. I only hope there are still some racehorses left to run on them.